TO THOSE LEFT BEHIND

This book is set in the typeface *Athelas* designed by Veronika Buri-
an and Jose Scaglione.

Hardcover ISBN: 978-1-0880928-66
Paperback ISBN: 979-8-3879173-70

A Publication of *Tall Pine Books*
119 E Center Street, Suite B4A | Warsaw, Indiana 46580
www.tallpinebooks.com

| 1 23 23 20 16 02 |

Published in the United States of America

DR. TRAVIS THOMPSON, LMFT

TO
THOSE
LEFT
BEHIND

HELPING PARTNERS *and* FAMILIES
UNDERSTAND AND HEAL
FROM ADDICTION

CONTENTS

Introduction ix

1. Therapy from Bob Newhart 1

2. Telling the Kitten Goodnight 35

3. Under His Eye 65

4. Thanks Nancy! 81

5. Per Jimmy Dugan 93

6. X&Y Track 4 119

7. And Three-Quarters, It Matters 137

8. Growing the Skylark's Feathers Back 159

9. Welcome to the Thunderdome 175

Conclusion 195

Meet the Author 199

Index 200

SPECIAL THANKS

This book would not be possible without my wonderful, beautiful wife Hannah. Without her, I would not be where I am. Her love and compassion have comforted, grown, and challenged me to become all that God created me to be. I will be forever indebted to her.

INTRODUCTION

MANY OF MY years have been in the midst of, or the wake of, addiction. From working in rehabilitation facilities, to working in private practice with couples in families, to housing foster children from parents with lifelong struggles with addiction, nearly every aspect of my personal and professional life sees the impact of drugs and alcohol. At first, there was a mix of a militant desire to "fix" those that seemed to have a screw loose. Then came the frustration that these people could not seem to stop, even while they tore their lives apart and the lives around them. I am nowhere near the end of my journey, but for now, I can honestly say that addicts hold a special place in my heart. Boundaries for my emotional health are difficult but necessary. It is a regular occurrence in my field to have clients past or present overdose and die. However, the love and compassionate curiosity that continues to develop has led to a steadfast goal of walking with whoever crosses my path. Alongside individuals, couples, families, and communities I hope to bring in a calm and confident challenge to what addicts, their loved ones, and culture expect of them. Recovery is possible.

ABOUT THE WRITING

I appreciate you taking the time to sit through my experience and theoretical musings. I hope this book provides you the ability to see and understand the dynamics of addiction in yourself, a loved one, or maybe even both. I will let you know that this book will involve a few different things. First, basic and somewhat complex topics will be discussed. Some of these things include psychological theory, terms related to addiction, and dynamics related to couples and families. All of these ideas will be broken down. I hope to not overwhelm anyone with what is in this book. It may be beneficial to stop and take time to process and discuss with someone.

Next, my thoughts and reflections will be given throughout. These will be denoted by a separate paragraph so that it is obvious there is a difference in discussion. Separate paragraphs will share reflections or struggles I have seen or experienced related to addiction and treatment. There will also be sparse sayings that I have picked up along the way or even used in my speaking or therapy sessions. Commentary may seem tangential or odd at first, but hang in there as things will be connected as this book goes on.

Finally, I will give hypothetical stories to aid in visualizing concepts and interactions, hoping they become real enough to relate to. These stories may be imaginary or include real people I have interacted with and walked with. So, if you see yourself or your situation in this book, take a minute and consider that addiction may not be all that special in nature. Patterns persist throughout all addictions whether they be chemical or behavioral. Some addictions contain specific concerns due to their lethality or unique circumstances, but take hope that if there is a pattern, there can be healing.

The last thing you will notice about this book is how my personality can seep through my writing. Please know that there is a difference between my writing, therapy, speaking, and interpersonal interactions. Do not expect that everything I say and theorize about addiction is spoken to clients. Some people are in a place of listening and some need to be listened to. I also tend to be a bit dry in my humor when speaking and writing. So, if it seems like I am being a heartless jerk who has no empathy for people, I might be.... Hopefully, you found humor in that last sentence, or this is going to be a long read for you. You will come across statements that I often repeat to clients when discussing certain topics related to addiction. These will be denoted throughout so that they can be used freely by readers. Do not worry, that part is free.

If words have escaped you in the past, the information in this book is here to help explain feelings and concerns around each subject.

What This Book Is

I am under no delusion that I have created or theorized brand-new information related to human development or interaction. Decades of research and experience came before me in the continual journey to peer into and aid in the human condition. So, any critique of an intervention, theory, or movement is done with great respect for what they have done, or what they may have earnestly attempted to do. However, this book does integrate ideas and theories that are not usually associated with addiction theory and treatment, along with continuations of ideas that are currently in place for treatment and recovery. For instance, developmental psychology often describes how mental health issues come to pass but does not often take its rightful place in understanding the growth of addiction.

The single most important motivation for this book is to help bridge the gap between what the latest psychological research says about understanding and treating addiction and what families and loved ones can interpret for use in their own lives. Put simply, I hope to make sense of the masses of information related to addiction and recovery in order to distill a palatable source of information accessible to anyone who needs it.

Here is the first instance of dry humor in the book. I am just placing this here to remind you that it will happen often. Did you get the joke? We are talking about alcoholics, and I used the word distill. Okay, I hope that prepares you enough for the rest of this endeavor. Good luck.

There is significant power in the knowledge of the chaos that you are experiencing. Life is a bit more bearable when circumstances can be understood and dealt with. Hopefully, this knowledge will allow you to feel confident and grounded in your experience, emotions, and next steps to gain help for yourself or someone you care about. It is also worth mentioning again that if I am speaking about the alcoholic husband, dynamics can generally be swapped for a drug-addicted wife. Some dynamics tend to fall off in connection when moving outside of chemical and alcohol addiction due to legal and health factors, but overall, clinical theory will remain intact.

WHAT IT IS NOT

At this point, I hope it is obvious this book is not a research-oriented document and will not qualify for any study in an academic journal. This is intentional. I will borrow from academia but do not wish to write another textbook. I hope you see the impact that knowledge in this area can bring. At the same time, this writing style comes with its limitations. This is not a comprehensive report on all aspects of addiction and the way it functions within individuals and those around them. At best, it is an incredibly intricate 30,000 ft view of the different facets of substance and alcohol abuse that could each qualify as their own literary work, which I may get to writing one day.

This book is also an entrance into further research or clinical practice. Implications and direct assumptions will be made but without the full theoretical and empirical background; it would be irresponsible to push past the boundaries listed here. Coupled with that, none of the information here should be expected to follow a treatment plan given by a therapist or loved one. While it is hopefully incredibly informative, the context in life experience and history always matters with addicts. What is incredibly impactful and helpful for one person could be toxic for another.

Finally, and most importantly, this book should not be used as ammunition. Concepts given in this book may completely revolutionize your perspective on addiction. In fact, some passages could "turn the lights on" when it comes to understanding yourself or a loved one. This is the hope for all treatment for families and loved ones of addicts. Please know, it would grieve my heart to have any of this work be used as a bludgeon to manipulate someone or coerce someone into treatment or therapy. Enlightenment in the area of relational dynamics can easily open up opportunities that otherwise seemed lost. Hope should not fuel resentment and revelation should not cause destruction.

THERAPY FROM
BOB NEWHART

IF YOU HAVEN'T noticed, the chapters here are not numerically named. This is not for some profound reason that should give you some great insight if you were to decipher where the ideas came from or how they relate to the topic. They are given these names because writing a book is a lot of effort, and they make me laugh when I read them.

Addiction identification and treatment have drastically shifted over the decades. From lambasting adult men for DUIs to needle exchange programs, the philosophies and interventions around addiction and recovery are vast. I could not hope to explore all of it here. It would be a much longer book that would take too much of my time and no one would read it. Instead, this chapter will go through an overview of the major movements in pursuit of sobriety. Some of these ideas will seem silly now, but at the time of their use, what was being done was likely "cutting edge" enough to become worthy of note. Their benefits and drawbacks will be examined as well. Some of these categories will be interconnected and are not chronologically listed, but they are organized in a way that should be straightforward enough to understand.

Moral Theory

The first overall category of addiction philosophy that we will look at is the Moral Theory. This collection of ideologies argues that addiction comes from an ethical or character flaw. In some cases, this can seem as fatalistic as it sounds. No addict can claim they are good, but only that they have some inherent flaw in them that needs to be adjusted, if it can be at all. Some groups attempt to address this moral concern through direct intervention and others in more collaborative work.

The shining example of total failure in curbing addiction and the consequences that result from it is Mothers Against Drunk Driving in their inception. They focused on criminalizing and demonizing all connections to alcohol and driving, even promoting complete abstinence that was fueled by emotional pleas. In hopes of shaming alcoholics into sobriety, submission, testimonies, and character assassinations in the early years of addiction research gave two certain outcomes. The first was the rise in blood pressure of anyone involved in either confronting alcoholics with DUIs or those that received backlash due to their continued impaired driving. Somewhat cathartic in the short-term, family members of those that died from a drunk driving accident could vehemently challenge those that continued to drink despite the consequences. The other surefire result of yelling at alcoholics is that it rarely does anything positive to their drinking patterns. Shame has proven to not be a constructive factor in the pursuit of long-term sobriety. That will be explored later.

Another attempt at utilizing a moral standard for staying away from drugs and alcohol is the DARE program. Wildly expensive and wholly ineffective, their mantra still sticks in the minds of Americans, "Just say no." To not belabor a topic that most have heard at some moment in their lives, the point of this saying is to build enough personal responsibility and pride in yourself to stop in the moment of being offered illegal substances or alcohol and be able to refuse. In other words, when someone offers you drugs, have enough pride and sense of value to turn around and leave.

Unfortunately, offering a moral position to a group of children and teenagers was predictably ineffective. DARE unintentionally offered insight into what treatment models and interventions need to be successful. To be truly beneficial, interventions must be understandable through the lens of those receiving them. Children and teenagers do not have the same understanding of consequences and morality. They think they are invincible. When a police officer or well-intentioned DARE employee shared about the dangers of drug use and how jail time could be connected, there was no ability to connect and reason as the understanding of long-term consequences is something that is developed much later in life. So, young people heard about how amazing drugs and alcohol could make you feel and simply disregarded the potential consequences as something that will happen to someone else. Since those early years, the DARE program has adapted, but the legacy still lives on.

It is incredibly obvious to therapists, psychologists, and researchers that you cannot make someone understand something that is outside their ability to see the world or imagine something different. Too bad government leaders sat upon a moral high ground in the rise of drug use instead of understanding how drug addiction functions. Too bad they made national changes about it as well.

Probably the most significant and influential organization and movement within a moral theory context is Alcoholics Anonymous. Before anything else is said about these amazing people, with all of their strengths and flaws, they are the only group I can think of that will willingly show up to get someone behind a dumpster at 3 a.m. on a Tuesday for free. They also have found reach through their "Big Book" across the world and hold meetings nearly everywhere and nearly every day. Great honor should be paid to these recovering addicts and alcoholics who paved the way for compassionate care for those suffering from addiction. Through the 12-Step program, many have found the ability to become and remain sober for weeks, years, decades, or even until their death. A community with tiered support is in place to aid anyone along the way. AA and its branches, such as Narcotics Anonymous, posit a significant reach and recovery record. So much so, that courts and other organizations will require individuals to attend meetings to maintain employment or as a part of parole requirements. They continue to modernize and attempt to remain current with a spiritual and non-traditional understanding of a higher power.

There are two concerns with AA. Those are its focus on the individual addict without the inclusion of the family as a parallel and inclusive member, and the decentralization of what AA is and its direction. There is a sister program to AA called Al-Anon that gives support to the loved ones of addicts, but it fails to include them in the process. This can unfortunately lead to the isolation of each member from the current process of recovery. Less known about AA culture, in general, is the 12 Traditions. For our purposes, Tradition 6 is worth focusing on. It prohibits AA from lending its name to outsiders for any reason other than invitation. This makes research and treatment utilization difficult as AA does not allow for outside influence or interference. To make things even more complicated, local chapters and meetings do not have the same expectations of behavior or social climates. These dynamics can vary from meeting to meeting and those seeking support from AA should consider many different meetings before concluding about its ability to help.

The last section of moral theory worth mentioning is that of spiritual interventions. This can include anything from involvement in religious organizations to the use of personal spirituality as a means of changing values. Religion and spirituality probably have the most significant variation in effectiveness and offensiveness for addicts. Some people have dedicated their lives to faith as a way to make sense of the world and find healing. Others have attended church twice, slept half the time, and wondered why they were not healed with an extra $20,000 in the bank by the end. Still, others report horror stories of members of the clergy using the concept of a higher power and eternity as a hammer to beat someone down with. Even more hold onto past pains and fears they experienced within a religious setting, making this category touchy to even discuss for some addicts. It is hard to pin down exactly what movements within a spiritual or religious context are most beneficial as they are so varied and scattered that any research would be sparse and highly presumptuous. It would urge you to be cautiously optimistic to use this approach blindly and would only consider active engagement with accountability to be worthwhile. Simply being associated with a faith or spiritual group does little to help in the plight of despair that is addiction. You do not get cured by sitting in the parking lot of an ER. Do not expect that any great work will be done in the half-hearted attempt to find healing.

Medical Theory

Any kind of true medical treatment or theory of functioning requires continual examination and revision. Years of research and evidence-based interventions are the foundation of any healthy and beneficial treatment. From this stringent adherence to study and application of understood phenomena comes both great knowledge and exploration of otherwise tragic conditions. Pure in ideology, the medical theory has suffered from two significant blunders in the realm of addiction, Overconfidence Bias and outright greed. There are a few things to remember as the medical model is examined in this book. Understand that this is not any call to abandon medicine or medical care, especially when necessary. If your appendix is about to rupture, do not hope that "right thinking" will cause it to repair itself. Go to the emergency room. If someone is suffering from alcohol poisoning, do not splash water on their face and assume they will be alright. Go to the emergency room. Instead, a cautious examination of the medical model and its progress is necessary to improve lives and medicine itself. Past theorists have assumed that addiction is like any other medical condition. Medical care is successful if symptoms are treated and managed. Still, many medical professionals hope for a cure but have resigned themselves to simply making sure their patient does not die in the next few days. Their frustration comes from this limited understanding of the individual, reducing them to symptoms that can be treated. This overconfidence in knowledge related to emotional and mental health has cost us dearly. Coupled with greedy pharmaceutical companies who fund and drive areas of research, a failure in response to addiction was all but assured.

Giving credit where it is due, the medical model helps in many different areas of health. Particularly in emergency rooms, the correct diagnostic process and care are necessary to retain life and support recovery. Carryover ideology from the treatment of heart attacks and broken bones bled into the adjacent rooms of addicts and alcoholics. Alcoholics keep showing up due to health issues and addicts keep overdosing, right next door to someone being admitted for a broken foot. It seems logical that these things would be treated similarly, especially if they are all in the same ER.

A general idea of the medical model is that addiction, like anything else, is a disease. Remember this word. If anyone talks about it being a disease, they are influenced heavily by the medical theories of addiction and will likely believe the following ideas. Addiction is seen in a similar vein as Type 1 Diabetes or cancer. There is some biological reason why someone would suffer from these things, and it is likely no fault of their own. Management of symptoms is key, and cures are hoped for. Once diagnosed, the rest of your life is forever changed. Type 1 Diabetes is chronic with maintenance and understanding needed to function with a nearly typical life experience. If treated, little consequences will arise. If neglected, your health degenerates very quickly. Cancer can go away, but the risk will always be there to come back, and regular checkups are needed. It can also come swiftly and with no warning, so awareness of self and potential symptoms are necessary. So, with medication and regular doctor's appointments, there is no reason why someone could not live a normal and healthy life. This is the assumption of how addicts could be treated as well.

Congrats! You are cured! Now, if you could just pay your deductible at the window on your way out, that would be great. If only it were that simple.

Following this model came with an opportunity. Addicts were coming through the medical system in droves and did not have treatment that could properly address their needs, only management of their immediate symptoms. The one thing consistent about addicts is their ability to continually need help. The greed of the pharmaceutical companies started to see this plight as an opportunity to marry the chronic treatment process of the medical model with inflated prices of medication. Fresh off of the investigations related to overprescribing stimulants and painkillers to patients that did not need them, was an opportunity to "help" in the problem they helped create. In comes medications like Suboxone and Methadone.

Side note here: there is plenty of information about the scourge of large pharmaceutical companies. While certainly a soapbox I could stand on for 30 pages, I will list some points here to get an understanding of why this has been such a problem. Early on, there was little information known about the addictive properties of opiates, also called painkillers. When this information became available to review, it was stuffed away in favor of selling pills like candy to charge insurance companies and gouge families of their income. Inevitably, stories came out about financial incentives companies offered doctors to not just prescribe these painkillers, but overprescribe them, such as the case in West Virginia where at one time there were 137 active pain prescriptions per 100 people. Either everyone in that state was hit by a bus all at once and then some, or corruption and greed stole life from everyday people.

Harm reduction models, while controversial, are the logical conclusion of the medical model of treatment. Basically, if addicts are going to use it no matter what we do, we might as well make it less bad. Initially, medications like Suboxone and Methadone were given as a taper, to lower amounts over time until they are no longer needed. This is a way to lower the use of opiates, or painkillers, by the general population over time. Unfortunately, this did not seem to work for a large portion of the people. Instead, a month-long taper turned into six months, a year, and then an indefinite amount of time. If these medications are inaccessible due to legal or financial concerns, then another option is available in the form of street drugs. If heroin addicts are going to continue to use a needle, then you might as well give them sterile needles to decrease the risk of transmitted disease through the sharing of used needles. If crack addicts can get diseases from old and dirty pipes, then offering them free and clean ones can reduce the risk of getting diseases from sharing a pipe. To the medical model, these people are terminally ill. Much like treating an end-stage cancer patient, palliative care is provided to at least make the process of dying more comfortable. They are going to probably die doing drugs, so we might as well do something.

Now comes the scary part. Emotions, relationships, and the mind do not work like that. Put simply, if you treat someone with medication that blocks opiate receptors, thus preventing overdose, they can just move to a stimulant like meth. They were cured of dying but will soon have a stroke. The good news is that you can hospitalize someone for the rest of their life and ensure that they never use meth as well. Clearly dripping with sarcasm here, the medical theory has become fatalistic. No cure for addiction can be found, so the goal is to throw treatment at someone and see what they take in. If it works and they are healed, then great! If not, then give them harm reduction and make them as comfortable as possible until they die.

Not to give an impression of complete resentment and denial of the progress that medical theory has brought us, but there are some shining lights to consider. While not a cure for addiction, medications that aid in anxiety, depression, mood regulation, and sleep have seen support alongside therapy as a way to give those in early recovery a fighting chance. Elements of recovery will be discussed later, but for now, understand that a world without substances to an addict is a terrifying one and any small aid can be vital. Also, honesty around use patterns has increased our understanding of mental and physical health issues. An easy connection is that of how drinking can affect the liver and levels of depression. If an alcoholic does not tell their doctor that they have been drinking and no tests are given to confirm this, then some strange occurrence must have happened to cause the issue. Someone may show depression because alcohol is a depressant. It makes you feel sadder and duller. There is clearly an interaction there.

There is one more benefit of medical treatment that is worth mentioning. This is the miracle drug known as Narcan. Able to pull someone from the depths of overdose on painkillers, this nasal spray has saved countless lives, with a catch. It was created and sold by the same pharmaceutical companies that gave fuel to America's opioid fire. They helped create a problem and are also selling a solution. Also, Narcan is only helpful if it is kept by those that do not use any drugs. This seems weird but makes sense. If an addict knows that they can use a ton of drugs and then get saved by someone with Narcan, then they can continue to increase their dose until the Narcan is not as effective anymore, thus leading to a more medication-resistant overdose. Everything with medicine should be balanced by the nuance of mental health. This is the crux of concern with the medical model: over-application of treatment past its effectiveness.

BEHAVIORAL THEORY

The next realm of addiction treatment has a long history in psychological research. Behaviorists were some of the early titans of psychology. Undergraduate students who took Psychology 101 will know about Ivan Pavlov and the training of dogs to salivate at the sound of a bell. A connection was made between a bell being run and being fed, causing the dog to start to anticipate feeding in which there was a biological response of drooling. This method of training is the cornerstone of training dogs today. The leap was then made possible for implementation on humans. With the right triggers and responses, behaviors could be molded into a beneficial outcome.

Another instance of behavioral training comes within a social environment. A different famous example of behavior and outside interactions affecting outcomes was in the study of Rat Park. Dr. Bruce Alexander took rats and placed them in isolation with the option to drink either water or water that was laced with cocaine or alcohol. Another set of rats was placed in a community of other rats with regular water and water mixed with drugs. The first set of rats that lived in isolation drank the contaminated water until it killed them. The rats that lived in the community and were allowed to fulfill all of their normal functions highly preferred the untainted water. What was remarkable about this study was just how different the results were from each group. It was then extrapolated that isolation, or reinforcement of disconnection, is a major factor in the use of substances, at least in rats.

For now, we will look at one last study about addiction and social reinforcers. This dates back to American soldiers in the Vietnam War. It is no secret that war is hell. Some may say it is worse than hell because it involves the suffering of innocent bystanders. This was increased by the psychological tactics that were used against soldiers. To cope with a drastic increase in stress and chaos around them, drug use skyrocketed. Heroin was cheap and easily accessible in Vietnam, so that tended to be the drug of choice. To get an idea of how bad the problem had gotten, the US government decided to do drug testing to compare the number of soldiers that tested positive before deployment with the number that tested positive while in Vietnam. Even with prior knowledge of a drug test coming, rates of positive drug results went from 11% in the US to 43% in the field of battle. Heroin-positive results skyrocketed from 2% to 34%. At the peak of military involvement, over 500,000 troops were active at one time. If we were to assume the worst and the previous percentages were used on the highest number of troops that returned, that would put over 200,000 soldiers positive for drugs, with over 170,000 of them using heroin. This was a meteor waiting to collapse the American medical system.

Instead, when the soldiers returned from the original study, the number of positive drug tests settled just above levels before deployment. Granted, some of those veterans moved to alcohol. Still, this was a baffling result. Whether due to boredom, trauma, disconnection, or something else entirely, a storm was brewing and then dissipated. Many researchers and psychologists attributed this change to social influences and support, much like Rat Park. There seemed to be proof that if addicts were just put in a supportive environment, they could recover. This point could easily be contended as soldiers returning from Vietnam were some of the most villainized individuals in the history of the US military. The overall idea of familiarity and family connection is what is important here, not the anti-war protests.

Rolling over from previous iterations of addiction treatment through a medical lens came the intervention process called Behavior Therapy. This has many versions such as Cognitive Behavioral Therapy, Dialectical Behavioral Therapy, and Acceptance and Commitment Therapy. They all come from the same premise that this section has been reviewing. If thoughts and behaviors could be changed, then outcomes could be changed as well. A common phrase for this is "fixin' stinkin' thinkin'." For most low-level concerns in mental health, such as panic attacks, anxiety, or depression, behavioral therapy can shift thought patterns to self-correct. This ties in with one of the greatest benefits of behavioral therapy, its ability to make immediate changes. Quickly seeing progress in reactivity in times that would have normally made someone anxious can bring a sense of progress and enlightenment. For some, this is enough. For insurance deductibles, this is good enough. This marriage between therapy and medicine has shaped practice toward insurance needs, rather than innovations in support of addicts. Insurance also is highly supportive of behavioral therapies due to the amount of research behind their theory and utilization. Partially due to the amount of time that behavioral theories have existed and partially due to recurrent funding of projects related to behavioral therapies, insurance and other medical entities hold this as the gold standard of nearly any treatment, alongside medication.

Behavioral therapies can suffer the same fate as medical theories of addiction. They can overestimate their effectiveness outside of the immediate context in which they are useful. Interventions are largely short-term and look for specific changes in the actions and beliefs of patients or clients. Unfortunately, the misread that the medical system makes about the ability to affect the rest of the life of an addict also applies here. So, now an addict does not follow through on feelings of wanting to drink. They pass every urine test for three months. Are they cured now, or did they just shift their behaviors to another area of dysfunction? Unless an individual allows for the expansion in the influence that behavioral interventions offer, then results can remain isolated. Some have even been able to game the system of mandated treatment by understanding the outcome that an evaluator is looking for and following through on "approved" behavior as long as necessary to avoid consequences. They will not smoke or use drugs until the test is complete, then go right back to what they were doing before. This is compacted by the highly individualized nature of behavioral therapies that do not include information and influence from significant others, families, or loved ones.

This reminds me of a time of volunteering in an outpatient treatment center during my internship for graduate school. There was a young woman who was in and out of treatment. She kept getting in trouble for using opiates, specifically heroin. Instead of following a program of abstinence, she understood what was expected of her in her behaviors and responses and changed her use to avoid punishment. All she had to do was pass drug tests. She adopted the use of fentanyl. This is an illegal drug that is much more powerful than heroin that also does not typically show on a drug screen. On paper, this woman was a successful patient who was thriving in outpatient treatment and was off all opiates and all other drugs as well. Instead, one of her peers snitched on her and said she was still using drugs, thus starting a process of dealing with relapse. Note, she started using fentanyl almost immediately upon admission into the program.

NEUROLOGICAL THEORY

Probably the most intriguing and confusing area of addiction research is how the brain is specifically affected, how neurology influences it, and how it is affected by the use of substances. I am no expert on this area of research but will hope to convey the important elements of neurology and its influence on addiction treatment. The basics that we will look at are the pathways that the brain takes, the structures of the brain, the chemicals that are important in the functioning of addiction, and the feedback that it gives the brain. Research and theories around how all of these things interact are constantly in flux. The more we learn about the brain, the more we understand that we do not know enough to make absolute claims about its functioning. There is just enough knowledge out there to make general assumptions about overall functioning and educated guesses about intricate functioning.

To make sense of the neurological functions of the brain, I will often use the metaphor of roadways. While not necessarily the best option for describing a three-dimensional structure of infinite complexity, it will get the job done. During fetal development and early childhood, the brain is both creating and connecting important sections of functioning such as speech, vision, memory, pain, decision-making, and even the ability to feel empathy. Consider these destinations as cities to arrive at and connect to others. In typical functioning, these cities will find ways to build pathways to one another, using innate ability and input from the outside world. If the city of sight needs facial recognition, and language for a baby to learn to speak, then roads must be planned, built, and maintained for them to travel into the skill of saying "dada." This journey happens so incredibly quickly and automatically that it is hardly noteworthy when the brain is not a topic of conversation. We are so used to learning ideas and skills that it is rare we ever consider how it comes to be.

At first, cities of the brain are connected by dirt roads and signs. There is a general direction to travel, but it is difficult and not consistent. Pathways are recognized and can be traveled, but there is hardly a highway built. Over time, one of two things can tend to happen. Connections are either strengthened by consistent and impactful travel, or they are abandoned. Either way, solidification in the brain is shown through use or deemed unneeded and discarded through synaptic pruning. Again, this is an oversimplification of neurological processes, but it is enough to grasp the idea of how the brain works through what is useful and what is not. When a pathway is considered to be both needed and useful, dirt pathways turn into rocky roads, into paved highways, and then into tracks for a bullet train. What once took a considerable amount of work to achieve moves into nearly effortless and instantaneous action. Much like the ability to move from one city to another is improved by travel innovation, so the brain also gains the ability to connect parts of the brain.

Now that we understand how things develop and go well, what happens if something is wrong with those connecting roads? Possibly one of the most saddening and comprehensive reports of neurological development and what happens when these roads are not built and maintained comes from the country of Romania. As the story goes, in the late 90s a researcher decided to look at the brain development of children at different levels of adoption from a local orphanage. This orphanage held a much greater number of children compared to the number of workers that could care for them. Not to any low view of the caregivers there, the number of babies and small children was simply overwhelming and only basic needs of survival were able to be met. It was a miracle they could achieve that. Thus, researchers were able to examine what would happen to a child if they were given basic needs but were deprived of the care and neurological feedback that is necessary for development. What was found was shocking and frightening. Children that remained unadopted for the longest showed the most significant gaps in brain structure and connection. They were simply missing roads between neurological cities. The ones that they did have were weak and hardly traveled. The cities themselves, centers of language, and decision-making, as well as many others, were also underdeveloped. The severe emotional neglect led to such a deficit in development, that these children were unable to follow through with basic skills such as problem-solving and emotional regulation. As they got older, these roads became solidified and, in some cases, were unable to be built or repaired. The absence of connection led to a literal deterioration of the brain. To put it simply, the longer a child was subject to neglect, the more likely it was that their brain was in disrepair that could never be recovered, even with loving parents and engaging social environments.

Through studies like this, as well as many other studies of the brain and development, there have been general theories about how the brain is divided and how each part functions. For our purposes, we will focus on three sections. The first is what is called the Reptilian section of the brain. Located at the base of the head and connected to the nervous system, the brainstem and the parts immediately connected to it represent automatic responses. Mostly involuntary, this portion controls things such as bodily functions that keep us alive, like blood pumping and nerves reacting to stimuli. The other function that it serves is to keep us alive when experiencing danger. Let's say for instance that you are walking through the Amazon rainforest, and a jaguar jumps out of a tree. Instead of wondering how many spots it has on its back or how white its teeth are, you will react out of fear and will automatically do what is necessary to remain safe. Whether you decide to fight, run, or sit still, the goal is to remain alive. In an instant, your brain has decided the best course of action to make it until tomorrow. Along with the immediate push to remain alive, other inputs are ignored, such as pain. If the jaguar is chasing you, it is of little consequence to have a cut on your foot. Many people report that in times of survival, they do not realize that they are bleeding until after they are safe, even to the point where broken bones do not cause pain for the time they are trying to stay alive.

The second part of the brain we will examine is the Mammalian section. This part focuses on the connecting aspects of social interaction. When we seek comfort or a sense of safety in a warm embrace, the Mammalian structures are active. Emotions and social queues are processed here as a way to interact with the community we are a part of. The pull for connection is also significant in the decision-making process of an individual. People can give up logical pursuits and safe interactions in favor of approval from a person or community. The need to belong to a group of people, also called a tribe, can both ward off psychological disorders, as well as cause them. For instance, individuals from broken homes can engage in behavior that is risky to their relationships, future, and body to find support and identity in a group. Even in typically "safe" environments, adults can sacrifice logical financial and legal decisions to feel loved and connected to someone. This connection also binds people together in an immensely positive way. Without care for one another, it would be difficult for anyone to succeed, as interconnection is necessary for future flourishing.

The last brain structure important to mention is the prefrontal cortex. Located at the very front of the brain, closest to the forehead, this section functions as our reasoning, risk management, self-control, and morality center. Much like other information we have learned about the brain, we understand some of the usefulness of the prefrontal cortex due to tragedy and loss of function. This time, a man by the name of Phineas Gage gives us information about what happens when this part is damaged. A railroad worker, Phineas was working on the tracks when a large metal rod was thrust through the bottom of his skull and out through the without killing him. Significantly damaging his frontal lobe, Phineas' personality immediately shifted, and his ability to handle emotions and make decisions was severely compromised. While function was somewhat regained over time due to the phenomenal flexibility of the brain, his accident showed us just how significant a loss of function could be when head trauma transitions into brain damage. The prefrontal cortex part of the brain is the last to develop, making it one of the final steps in development. It is understood that the brain grows from the base upward. Expansion and complexity are built over time, with the final overall construction ending at the prefrontal cortex at around age 25. Now, some have taken this to mean that anyone younger than 25 is not responsible for their actions because their brain is not fully developed. This is misinformed and kind of stupid. Just because a city is not fully completed does not mean that it is uninhabitable. Interstate 24 has been under construction since I was a child and people still drive on it like they are making their NASCAR debut, and Nashville is constantly updating with too many people there already.

With all of these parts of the brain in mind, there is one more thing to consider, and that is plasticity, or the ability of the brain to adapt to needs and changes. Using our road analogy again, if a pathway is considered highly traveled and needed, updates and streamlining will take place. If very few people travel a road anymore, it may become run-down and harder to travel on. However, if something should happen to a road and it is no longer drivable or is so overcrowded that it becomes impractical, alternative routes can be created. Just how possible is it to do this rewiring? It depends on a few things. First, age plays a significant role in how adaptable the brain can be. The consequences are more significant when someone is young as growth and development are a part of the natural process. Just like a road, an open landscape is ripe for growth. Once it has been carved and paved, less can be done to change the overall design as time moves along. Instead, creative adaptations are needed to change the flow of traffic and increase travel times. Another important factor that influences the brain's ability to adapt is the motivation of the person hoping to change it. A way that this can be is the difference between someone who learns a new language for a grade in school and someone who learns a new language to pursue the "love of their life." Simply shoving information into someone's ears is not enough to cause lasting change. The brain has short and long-term functions and can dump information that is deemed unnecessary. Just ask anyone who has been a student at the mercy of standardized testing. Many other aspects of brain development will influence plasticity, but these are the parts that are useful to us now.

Other than the structural parts of the brain, there are chemical interactions that influence everything from emotion, to love, to pleasure. There are untold numbers of these chemical interactions, but they generally work like this. Each chemical is a message. They tell other parts of the brain what is happening and what responses to give. Specific chemical messages are given for love, connection, and even stress. Ideally, we could see which chemicals are over or under-communicating and determine what a person is missing to feel "normal." From there, we could even give them the perfect medication to solve all of their issues. If only it were that easy.

The final important part to consider when thinking through the neurological impact of addiction is the natural functions of the brain itself. While infinitely complex and still incredibly opaque in observation, some basic assumptions permeate all matters of processing. The main goal of the brain is to stay alive. Nothing else is important to consider if you are dead. Next, running all of these intense functions simultaneously requires intense efficiency. To achieve this, the brain will make shortcuts and solidify pathways that are used and supported. This is incredibly useful when needing to drive, and road conditions can change in an instant. No one thinks about all of the steps that come with driving; we just do them. If we did not, no one would get very far out of their driveway before they were late to work. Imagine having to think through every single step it took to make a car work without crashing. Alongside that need for efficiency, pathways that are already established will be connected to future stimuli. Once a child learns the name of their dog, they often assume that every dog has the same name. Until they learn the difference, this generalization is the default. The last overall function of the brain important here is the capacity to use certain abilities at specific points. A hilarious misunderstanding of brain function is that people only use 10% of their brains. This is crazy, but understandable if you do not know exactly how the brain works. Okay, let us use another metaphor as a comparison. Did you know that a generic stoplight only uses one-third of its light at a certain time? Wouldn't it be great if it used all the lights at once? No, it would not. Just the same with the brain. Instead of causing major collisions and insurance headaches, a brain activated all at once is having a seizure. Positive outcomes are all about using what is necessary and useful.

After that crash course in neurological theory and development, let's apply this to how an addict's brain functions. When an addict is in active cycles of use and abuse, a few things are notable about their brain function. First, the prefrontal cortex is dark. Decisions are made day to day about gaining the substance of choice, how to use it, and how to hide it from those that would make them quit. Unfortunately, little brain activity is utilized to engage in morality, consequences, and problem-solving. In effect, we can see through brain scans that those in active addiction are not utilizing their capacity to think through consequences and the next steps, let alone how to engage in a sense of integrity and sacrifice. The ability is still there, but the city has been slowly abandoned over time, allowing for breakdowns in communication, safety, and travel. Particularly in the more severe cases of addiction, individuals hardly have any capacity for logical processing of long-term needs or consequences. Morality is overrun by the need to get the next fix.

The Mammalian section of the brain also begins to lack. Some connections are needed and continue, but those tend to be ones related to access to resources instead of genuine relationships for the benefit of both parties. Connection of social needs begins to become tied to the Reptilian part of the brain, focusing on relationships with bonds in intensity comparable to life-and-death situations. Emotions become volatile without the regulation of the prefrontal cortex. Again, without the grounding of long-term consequences, what is immediate is what is real. Unfortunately, this dysregulation can only last so long without resolution, leading to a need to use substances to satisfy the emotional outrage and disconnection that comes from living life impulsively.

The final section, the Reptilian part, is the most active of the three. In constant activation, this automatic life-saving feature is not just on, but always in overdrive. Instead of using fear and panic as temporary tools to achieve safety, addicts cannot seem to drop their levels of stress and panic. Just as was mentioned before, the brain likes efficiency and will try to use the same road as much as possible. So, if it worked to freak out when feeling withdrawal symptoms and a reward was given for use of a substance, then the brain will deem it appropriate to continue to use this route. Since this part of the brain is the most automatic, it can be the most difficult to intervene on and change. The addict then continues to use it to "survive" until it kills them.

The chemical messengers can also cause havoc in the addict's health and recovery. Three of these are important to keep track of: cortisol, dopamine, and oxytocin. The first of this triad, cortisol, is the chemical communicator for stress. When active, the brain shifts to a high alert with every decision requiring urgency indicative of life and death scenarios. The second is dopamine, every addict's true love. Dopamine is that feel-good chemical that we get from chocolate, sex, and high amounts of drugs. Oxytocin, not to be confused with Oxycontin, is the connection or "cuddle" hormone that binds people together. Addicts tend to show an increased level of cortisol, crazy changes in the amount of dopamine, and little oxytocin. So how does this play out? Continued high levels of cortisol tell the brain to continue to be stressed and anxious. When there is nothing immediate to be anxious about, then addicts assume that danger is hidden somewhere they cannot seem to find it. Dopamine is either bottomed out or skyrocketed in addicts, which I will come back to. Oxytocin becomes a rare commodity as connection takes a backseat to survival. Due to the brain's desire to remain efficient, little is accessible during active use.

Now to dopamine, the chemical we all chased after in our addiction. It is helpful to think of dopamine intake as a tank. A "normally functioning" adult has a moderate amount of dopamine, nothing too high or too low. They sit in the middle, signaling to the brain that everything is stable, and no real action is needed. Natural activities such as eating chocolate or laughing at a joke can raise the amount of dopamine in the tank temporarily, to which it returns to its normal levels. Other activities such as sex can significantly increase levels of dopamine, which then end up leveling out. However, drugs do something far more effective. In the "first hit," as it is called, the dopamine tank is overflowed to a degree in which it cannot handle. The brain, with all of its wisdom, realizes that there seems to be free dopamine being offered and it does not have to make as much on its own. So, it decides that it should make less than the natural amount as the addict will supply the rest. This creates a problem where the addict has to use more of the same substance to achieve a similar effect, and so it goes on. Cycling through dopamine overflow and adjustment, the addict finds themselves at a crossroads. They could get off drugs, but the result would be a brain that panics due to not having the natural dopamine levels needed to feel stable. This is where the phenomenon comes from when addicts talk about not using to get high but using to feel normal. They need drugs to get to a "normal" level of dopamine that non-addicts feel every day.

Now, you as an addict are properly screwed with no true end in sight. Family members and loved ones will ask you to just stop using drugs or alcohol. What they do not understand is that the brain has slowly taken away the ability to choose. What is missing is the belief that doing something different will not kill you, and that everything does not fall apart if you stop. They do not seem to get that every waking moment is either seeking after a drug or trying to enjoy some semblance of peace that comes from using it in a life that seems to be drowning in despair. It is of no use to try to explain it to them. They will think you are making up another excuse, and most of the time you are to hide your shame. You say insane things all the time to get people off your back. I mean, come on. How many times can one man get the flu in three months? At some point, you run out of excuses.

Going back to our roads and cities analogy, work can be done, but it has to be strategic. The connections made through active addiction are incredibly strong. So much so that it is a miracle if those connections ever leave. Many addicts who have relapsed will state that when they did go back to using, it was as if nothing had changed. Instead of trying to repave over the roads of addiction, we need to do two things: create roadblocks and make detours. The ability to be an addict may never leave, but it is possible to make so many roadblocks it is nearly impossible to ride on the highway to hell. Some of these roadblocks will be family connections, goals in life, or even the belief that life has meaning. Engagement in oxytocin-involved activities can create detours. As powerful as pain and suffering are, with a purpose it seems as if we can avoid negative reactions. Just ask the mother who watched her child leave the womb, and ask if she is feeling pain, or speak to the father who shielded his family from the impact of a tornado, and ask if fear and costs were a limiting factor. Making detours is difficult as past connections are overgrown and need consistent work to find a new connection. Cities may have become run-down and decrepit. Repairs can happen, and time can aid in recovery. It will take practice and consistent effort, but alternate routes can be found, and chemical imbalances can either be adjusted naturally or aided through therapy and possible medication.

All of this information is in continual flux. We are learning more and more about how the brain works, but we are also learning how incredibly complicated it is. It is not likely that everything listed here will be outright refuted, but new data could easily give clarification we did not know we needed. There is one flaw in this drive to understand the brain—determinism. If you are not sure what that is, it just means that how you are wired is how you are fated to be. A valiant attempt but ultimately disproved, our genes heavily influence us, but they do not assure us who we will be as human beings. There is some flexibility. For instance, I will never be an astronaut. My parents lied to me. I cannot do whatever I set my mind to. No matter how much I work and what I accomplish, I am too tall to fit in the cockpit. On the other hand, I can alter my responses to situations and work on the way that I respond to outside interactions. That means that I may not be able to be an astronaut, but I can write a book. You may also have heard about the alcoholic gene or addict wiring in the brain. Again, a valiant idea, but no hard evidence. We have not found a gene, and neurological wiring can be cloudy and subjective.

ATTACHMENT THEORY

Full disclosure here: this is my favorite lens of addiction work. Take a break if needed to have a fresh mind when reading this. The next few pages may hold some understanding of why addicts do what they do under unthinkable circumstances, as well as explain the reasons why someone uses drugs and alcohol in the first place. This may make me sound like an oracle or something. That is certainly not the case; just ask my beloved wife who often corrals my wild ideas. Instead, look into the following information as a collaboration of decades of research and centuries of philosophy in the understanding of the human condition.

Why should you believe me in this? Because I'm right and have the fancy letters at the end of my name. Man, I'm hilarious. Even writing this now, I have a smile on my face.

Anyway, let me explain the theory and how it can open the door to understanding the needs that are attempting to be met through addiction. Then, you can decide for yourself if this helps bring light to you or someone you care about. Buckle up, 'cause here we go.

Our story begins in the late 60s with researchers by the names of John Bowlby and Mary Ainsworth. At this time in psychological research, there were competing theories about how children develop over time and the ways that they form relationships and connections with caregivers. From this previous research, Bowlby and Ainsworth each held beliefs about the experience of attachment in children and the bonds they form with caregivers. Through various interactions and professional relationships, they were able to collaborate and form a new effort in the search for an understanding of how human relationships come to be. Their most famous experiment in pursuit of this endeavor was called the Strange Situation.

The experiment was fairly straightforward to replicate, and all observations are made from behind a one-way mirror. The process and results are so fascinating, there have been multiple recreations that have been videoed and posted online. The Strange Situation includes three different people. There is the mother and her child, as well as a stranger. To start, the mother and her child sit in a room and play together. Once the child is settled and comfortable, the mom leaves the room. Once she leaves, the child will typically begin to cry as they have been left alone. Then, a stranger will come in and attempt to console the child, usually to no avail. Next, the stranger leaves the child and the mother returns to the room to help her child calm down. What happens as the mother returns and attempts to embrace the child is the main focus of the study.

Once all of these responses were coded and organized, there were three general responses that children gave their mothers. The first group, deemed securely attached, contained children that were sad when the mother left and were able to be consoled when she returned. These children were able to return to play with the mother in the room and seemed to feel safe in the room again. The second group, deemed insecurely attached, was split into two separate classifications. The first was insecure-anxious. These children were upset when their mother left but were not able to be fully soothed when she returned. Some continued crying past the point of normal regulation and others seemed to "punish" mom for leaving. They would even hit or push away when she attempted to hold them. Other children in this section were labeled as insecure-avoidant. These kids showed little regard for their mother leaving and returning. Almost seeming flat, these children did not display any particular connection to having their mother leave and come back. Nearly all of the children could be placed in these three categories. There were a few children that seemed to fluctuate between categories and were labeled disorganized.

Theories then began to emerge about what each category meant and how each child got to the point where they gave the responses that they did. Some assumed that everything was inherent in the child's brain, while some gave ideas about behavioral training. As more data was gathered, a larger picture began to form around the interactions that mothers regularly had with their children. Children with secure attachments tended to have mothers who were able to provide consistent care and support in all aspects of interaction. While not perfect, they were responsive to the emotions and needs of the child and provided the appropriate response to validate and allow them to move on. Children with insecure-anxious attachments tended to have mothers that were largely inconsistent with their reactions to emotional needs. At some points, they would be heavily invested in supporting their child. Other times, children were dismissed or outright ignored. This created an environment in which a child was unsure about what response they would get. The children with insecure-avoidant attachments, like their securely attached peers, also experienced consistency in maternal interaction. Unfortunately, the consistent reaction of mothers in this group was neglect. The children learned that their caregiver was highly likely to not tend to their needs. Thus, they developed a capacity for self-resolution and did not often take outside emotional input.

I am going to put a small excerpt here to hopefully calm some fears that can come from reading this information. The Strange Situation was created and pioneered at a time when psychologists were obsessed with the mother-child bond. Exclusivity in results is more related to the population studied, not the real world. A child's father may provide a drastically different attachment to their child than the mother. Please do not assume that the maternal bond is the end-all-be-all of childhood development.

Once this research reached a large enough audience, researchers began to wonder how these attachment styles continued and how they would play out in long-term behavior. With continued curiosity, there were interesting trends and concerns. First, it was discovered that the attachment style was not fixed. Sure, there was a likelihood to continue what was known, but children were able to shift towards secure attachment with adjustments to environment and parenting. Also, different attachment styles showed tendencies towards different issues. Securely attached children were the most likely to have positive mental health reports and healthy, intimate relationships. Adults with an insecure-anxious attachment style were most likely to have mental health disorders and inconsistent emotional relationships. Those with insecure-avoidant attachment showed low engagement in intimate social interactions and were not likely to pursue outside input. It became apparent that these adults had developed adaptations to their upbringing and learned from their experiences in the world. The usefulness of these changes is up for discussion, but it was incredibly clear that these adults were a product of their upbringing.

Upon further examination of the connection between children and their caregivers, another trend began to emerge. There were core goals that were being met by the behaviors of children, even throughout their lifespan. When children were younger, these were more obvious. As we have continued to observe and theorize, there is a belief that our needs do not change, but they simply become more metaphorical over time. The four Basic Needs were identified and labeled Safe Haven, Secure Base, Proximity Maintenance, and Separation Distress. The Safe Haven is the place that a child would run to when they felt scared. This is where you go to feel safe and protected. Like a shelter in the rain, a Safe Haven allows someone to let their guard down and recharge. This is seen when a small child will look for the comfort of a caregiver when a stranger comes around. A Secure Base is like an information center and launching pad. It is what we use to make sense of the world, how we interpret new ideas, and the way that we get the basics of what we need to be successful. A child asking about a new idea or looking for approval when starting a new hobby encapsulates this. Proximity Maintenance is how someone can mitigate feeling disconnected from their safety. The playground is an obvious example of when children will check to see if their parents are still there, or they look around to ensure that their parents are paying attention. The final need, Separation Distress, is how an individual copes with continued distance. When a child is dropped off at daycare and starts crying, there is nothing they can do to make their caregiver return. Instead, they must learn the skills necessary to be temporarily disconnected from their parents that make sense of the world.

Once a child becomes a little older, there is a shift in how these four Basic Needs are met. The focus of resolution moves from the parents or caregivers to friends. Now, when something bad happens, the adolescent will speak to their friends to calm them down, ensuring a Safe Haven. They will hear the opinions of their peers and role models to develop a new worldview, creating a new Secure Base. They also learn more abstract ways to deal with Proximity Maintenance and Separation Distress. In today's world, cell phones and social media become a stand-in for face-to-face attachment needs, with lessened positive results. Teenagers will often connect with their friends to "see what they are doing" in hopes of continuing connection. Separation Distress is probably the most obvious and sometimes hilarious (from an outside perspective) need that is met. A young couple that finds the person of their dreams at 14 years old can often say in the school hallway, "I'll see you next period, and don't be late," or "Why didn't you respond to my text as fast as you normally do?" While immature and funny to witness, these children are growing their understanding of interpersonal connection and what they can tolerate when distance comes between them and someone they care for.

In adulthood, the givers of Basic Needs again shift, this time from friends to significant others. In this dynamic, the partner provides the physical and emotional connection to feel as if the world is calm again with just a hug. A Safe Haven can also be in a significant other telling their partner that things will be okay and to take a breath. A Secure Base is established in the desire to define a relationship and understand where the other person is coming from. Making sure that there are no secrets is important here as, without a Secure Base to stand on, it can feel as if an identity has been taken away. Proximity Maintenance then becomes more symbolic at this stage, with agreements and gestures often standing in the place of literal plans and interactions. Individuals can be soothed with the belief that their partner will be there for them at the end of the day, even if they are not able to answer the phone at the moment. An increased amount of grace is given as life becomes more complex. Finally, Separation Distress continues in symbolism and maturity with the possibility of both partners working and not being in the same location. A simple text reminding you about dinner or a heartfelt card can be a stand-in for future joining.

When these potentially healthy attachments go awry, then an opportunity for dysfunction begins to creep in. Some people respond to the lack of connection through desperation, engaging in risky relationships with ease of access in response to a fear that they will be alone. Others will be marred by persistent suspicion of others, finding themselves alone and unable to be truly connected to anyone. Here is the first instance in this book where you can see that addiction is not all that special. It seems to be that every lens of addiction seems to come with an exception. The moral model will establish a spiritual or cultural context for support, but it will fail to reach those that desperately want to change. The medical model aids in recovery, but ultimately cannot help someone heal from actual hurts they have experienced. Sure, we can train someone through a behavioral model, but what happens when behaviors change and people do not? The brain is a wild and wonderful frontier, but it leaves us with questions about how it even makes things work or how people seem to defy their wiring. Attachment Theory somewhat subverts this idea. While it could be that continual emotional rejection could have led to an addicted person, it also posits that feelings of abandonment, without strict and literal evidence, could produce the same results. Attachment Theory simply reflects on the beliefs that arose from experience without needing a literal genesis that launched someone into cycles of drug abuse.

To find out if attachments have anything to do with addiction, we will apply previously mentioned ideas and see if they translate into addiction both in its study and in the experiences of those that have experienced it. I will also include some of my experience as a therapist and researcher to clarify important points. Let's start with attachment styles. Leaning back to our previous discussion about outcomes related to how children were securely attached to their mothers, children with the highest rates of concern later on in life were not the secure or insecure-avoidant ones, but the insecure-anxious ones. Their belief of the world, shaped by caregivers that provided varying levels of support, showed that life is unpredictable. Sometimes people will be there for you, and without warning, they may abandon you. Taking some liberty here, those that are not able to resolve this issue need a way to cope. This is not where drug and alcohol use comes from. That is a couple of steps later. Instead, desperate attempts for connection are made with heightened levels of stress and anxiety. There are two things to consider here. Anxious people do not always make the best rational decisions, and perpetually anxious people do not make the best partners. Partially due to their fear of loss and due to their lack of self-value, nothing can be certain. It is more advantageous to be on guard than to be comfortable because if you are unaware, you will get hurt and not be prepared for the fallout. This is where addiction can start to seep in. A synthetic alternative to a failure in connection through vulnerability, substance use provides a short-term solution. They can fill in the gaps of these inevitable breakdowns, offering hope to alleviate the feelings for a short time.

By default, addicts suffer from a long-term insecure-anxious attachment. Again, this is not an indictment of parenting roles or a search for specific trauma. Instead, there is a consistent belief that the world is unstable. The more intensely the person feels this loss, coupled with how long they have been experiencing it, helps us understand two things. The first is how someone can "suddenly" become addicted to a substance. There has been a history of not feeling safely attached to those that are needed. After being worn down, eventually, there is a shift that happens from attempting to reconcile fear to needing to feel safe somehow. In this substitution, there is consistency. Alcohol will never abandon you. It will drain and isolate you, but it will never leave you. Second, it speaks to the resulting failure of the connection itself. It is not that alcohol is better, it is just there and always will be. Whether that is due to a disconnected spouse, or it is just a general mistrust from previous experiences, is something to explore in therapy. Either way, addiction is bred and maintained by failure to find safety and attachment. It is the result of an inability to feel safe in someone's arms or assured in promises. It is the desperation of coping with loss and feeling alone.

The four Basic Needs also can be met through substances. The Safe Haven is probably the most obvious in its translation. When a fight breaks out between someone and someone they care about, what do they do? Instead of working it out or talking with a friend, they decide to go drink about it. That is a Safe Haven. Synthetic Safe Havens provide something that organic and human interactions do not; complete and total consistency in response. Addicts and alcoholics can even tell you how much they need to use or drink to feel a certain way. Even down to the ounce or gram, there is a science to just how much is needed to feel okay, to feel safe. The insidious effect of engagement in a synthetic Safe Haven is that it overpowers and rejects other natural forms of connection. Nothing is as good or as reliable as whiskey is. Drugs invalidate other forms of safety, making them seem useless and unable to support the addict. You simply cannot out-hug heroin.

Addiction's Secure Base is more noticeable over time. After repeated engagement with a drug or alcohol as a Safe Haven, a new perspective on life and needs begins to form. Not only do substances solve the problem of needing to run away, but they also can morph someone's point of view into making sure they are within the realms of use. Consider this almost like a cult. Once you are in, the cult and its leaders will tell you about the world, how it works, and what you need to do to remain safe. Over time, nearly every aspect of your life is viewed through the lens of the charismatic leader. Your thoughts rarely become your own. They start to mix so much with what you have been told, that it becomes difficult to differentiate between what you think and what you are told to think. When someone who says they care about you tries to convince you that the fountain of joy and serenity is somehow a sham and that you are too ignorant to see the big picture, all they sound like is someone who wants to steal joy from you.

Proximity Maintenance and Separation Distress become immediately apparent when the drug or alcohol is needed or will be needed in the future. If we remember that Proximity Maintenance is the tempering of the distance between an individual and their representative sense of safety, then we can simply apply addiction and see what happens. Another way to measure addiction through an attachment theory lens is how necessary the person finds it to be close to their alcohol or drug of choice. Do they plan their day around the ability to use? Are they constantly concerned about having their phone charged to message a dealer or their keys to be able to drive to the liquor store? Addicts will begin to stress when becoming distant from their attachment needs. They may create chaos to remain close enough to their ability to use, while also maintaining beneficial relationships. Addicts will then panic if they are separated either through force or coercion from the ability to access substances. A family gathering that will be lengthy in time or an arrest can easily set off alarms for them.

Separation Distress is triggered by a biological and psychological response. When withdrawal symptoms start to hit or the high begins to wear off, an addict will find themselves beginning to plan, often urgently, to reconnect with their sense of safety. Whether through shaking, sweating, or "having the flu," addicts will panic and plan to connect to their drug of choice. Interestingly enough, soothing feelings of Separation Distress is one of the greatest pushes against a pure behavioral or neurological medical model. There is a simple test to see if addiction has truly enveloped someone and captured their psyche. When they feel the need to use and they are either on their way to get drugs or alcohol, or they know it is coming to them, addicts will start to feel better. While it seems wild that a heroin addict can go from intense panic and fear into hopeful anticipation without a substance, addicts will often report this. Just like when a crying child sees their parent walk towards them and begins to calm down, so does the addict with their dealer on the way.

With all this psychological terminology out of the way, let us translate what this means into something we can all understand. Put bluntly, addicts have slowly sold themselves. Their soul has slowly been bartered away for a fleeting sense of safety. What was once a reprieve from daily suffering has turned into a marred sense of comfort that will eventually kill you. Addicts have put aside what is healthy, needed, and vulnerable, and connected themselves to a synthetic attachment. Alcohol requires no vulnerability, no submission. There is nothing to fear and nothing to risk. Cocaine will always give that feeling, that rush, of the world making sense. Meth will constantly be able to take away all of the horrors and hurt that someone has experienced, opening a new world where life is engaging and pain is not an option. Like that warm blanket on a cold night, substances make you feel safe and at home.

Unfortunately, this safety comes at a cost. Addiction will isolate people and have them believe that there is no one else that can make them feel the smallest sense of safety that alcohol does. To some degree, addicts know this. They understand that their drug is not enough. They know that no matter how much they use, they will never fully be comforted again. Sadly, this is all they can seem to access, all they can hope to reach for. The daily selling of their soul for a synthetic embrace has cost them everything, and only it remains to be there when they fall again. No one is there to save them. No one could possibly bridge that gap from a barren soul to a life worth living. It is all gone, and they have made it that way.

We will talk about treatment and how to make progress in both immediate intervention and the process of recovery. However, I would like for you to take a moment and take in what you just read. Many people have heard of addiction as a choice that someone makes as if they decided one day to abandon their children and spend their entire life savings in a week. Granted, small choices are made along the way that lead to an avalanche, but if you are not an addict, please hear the desperation in that last paragraph. In my work with addicts in both short-term and long-term efforts, no one has ever truly disagreed with me. Some have given pushback because reaching that deeply into someone's soul can be jarring. Still, addicts find themselves alone and abandoned. They know they have done this to themselves, but they see no other option. Their lives have become a total sham, propped up by the rotten foundation that barely keeps them breathing, and they know it.

Before we move on to the next chapter, please take a moment to appreciate what you are about to read. It brings sorrow to my soul to write these next sentences, with real-life grief playing through, knowing what absolute pain it is to heal these decrepit attachment wounds. This is what it feels like to attempt recovery. We know that addiction provides synthetic safety and addicts have sold the real thing for the fake one over time. They have not just sold comfort to the slave driver of addiction. Instead, what they once thought was a minimal compromise was a small piece of their soul. As time went on, what was assumed to be small, became not so. What was a son's missed football game on a Friday night was actually the last shred of hope he held out for his father to return. The small brush to the side of his wife's needs built into her a sense of fear, resentment, dread, despair, and then apathy. Addicts have not only sold away connections but their humanity. What has made them a person has drifted so far away, that there is nothing left but the mirage of misguided hope and desperation.

Taking away this wretched compromise, to demand someone to embrace sobriety is asking them to face the horrors of an empty soul, awaken to a desolate relationship landscape, and recognize that the only identity they have left is to be sick, to be empty. In the most severe cases, addiction has taken away everything someone held dear, corroding their very sense of self. To take away alcohol now is to steal the only identity they have left, the only thing tethering them to a quaking ground. Like jerking someone out of a hot tub in the middle of a snowstorm, so is the demand for recovery. To live without the risk of overdose or poisoning, there is a requirement to give up the one last thing that makes sense. Sobriety is the unending endeavor of peering into a barren soul, embracing the despair, and having some small hope that there is something on the other side. After years of seeing all this abhorrent and distressing view on life, I can say, it is worth it.

There is hope.

TELLING THE KITTEN GOODNIGHT

THERE ARE MANY different ways to understand mental health. Just as there are so many theories of addiction, there are many about mental health disorders and symptoms. To some, there are arbitrary lines that are drawn in treatment modalities and diagnoses. For others, there is a strict code of treatment and processing issues. Like most things in life, the best solution is probably somewhere in the middle. As someone in psychology field, it can seem like everyone has come up with the magic pill that will fix everything. Six months later, there is a better one. As someone who has received treatment for mental health, it can feel like a cacophony of salesmen all espousing their miracle cure. There is snake oil everywhere. I hope to cut through some of this stuff and make the understanding of mental health a little more accessible for you.

Treatment of mental health in addiction is incredibly complex. We will look at the interconnection between mental health symptoms and substance use throughout this chapter. There is something important to understand before moving forward. Substances throw a wrench in everything. Addiction can mimic so many things that diagnoses require truth about sobriety to remain valid. In addiction, someone can even qualify for a mental health disorder, even if the drug itself is what is causing the issue. Truth and investigation are required to make any sense of mental health in addiction.

No matter where you fall at the end of this chapter, I hope you hear some form of humanization of the struggles of mental health and addiction. There will be challenging aspects to this that will push against commonly accepted beliefs. While nothing radical, I will hope to fill in the gaps that are often left open to keep addicts and their families sick. There is a way forward, no matter the diagnosis or substance.

DIAGNOSES

It should be said before this chapter goes any further that what you will read should not be taken as direct medical or clinical advice. This chapter exists to help make sense of the incredibly complicated nature of mental health and addiction. While you do not get a diploma after reading this book, you certainly can get a better perspective on how psychological diagnoses come into play.

We can start with everyone's favorite question about mental health and addiction: Which came first, depression or addiction? Was it the low feelings that drove him to drink, or is it the drinking that caused him to feel so depressed? When I was first asked this question as an inexperienced therapist, I took time to explain complexities, consider perspectives, and tried to gain a history from the family so that I could answer correctly. My answers got better over time. At this point, I have gotten tired of that and have started to be honest. So now when a client or their loved one asks me: Which came first, the depression or the addiction? I then answer: I have absolutely no idea. If uncle Jacob is sneaking airplane bottles of whiskey to a tee-ball game, I really don't care either. There is little point to make a great guess of what exactly started the addict in addiction if they are currently in it.

Why is this a problem? Can we not just look at their symptoms, play Bingo with diagnostic categories, and find the perfect way to fix them? No, we cannot. This is our first problem in diagnosing mental health disorders in addiction. There is no way to tell what the result of addiction is, what is the result of the long-term effects of addiction on the body, and what predated addiction itself if an addict is in the middle of a binge. Unfortunately, many who are reading this book have experienced well-intentioned mental health experts just trying to get a label to help and not-so-well-intentioned mental health experts that seem to have the answers of someone's life from a fifteen-minute interview. The medical model that came into play in the previous chapter rears its ugly head here. It states that a correct understanding of symptoms can lead to effective treatment. That only sort of works, even for purely biological processes.

The short-sightedness of many practitioners has muddied the water for so many people. Let me give you a real-life example. For a bipolar diagnosis, I will highlight some symptoms that will be important to remember. I have had many clients that show symptoms of a bipolar diagnosis in both manic and depressive phases, the emotional highs and lows. In their manic phases, they have felt inflated self-esteem, decreased need for sleep, racing thoughts, an increase in goal-directed activity, and engagement in risky behavior. During their depressive phases, they feel a low mood most of the day, loss of interest in anything, fatigue, feelings of worthlessness and guilt, and cloudy thinking. Now, if you were to look at these symptoms, it is abundantly clear that there is some chemical imbalance in the brain of this person. Their moods are wild, and they need medication to regulate them. There is something wrong with their brain wiring and will need time to learn new skills to cope with the mood swings. Or, you know, they are using a ton of meth. That explains all of those symptoms.

I know that I am oversimplifying here, but I cannot tell you how many addicts have come into my office in both residential treatment and private practice with that diagnosis. It must be annoying at this point because it borders on incompetence in some of the people handing out medication. Why would a psychiatrist give a diagnosis of bipolar if the addict is using meth? One reason is that the psychiatrist did not ask or push hard enough. The other is that the addict did not tell them. Whenever an addict tells me they have a diagnosis of bipolar, the next thing I ask is did they tell their psychiatrist about the meth use? They usually say no. Here is another huge issue in diagnosing mental health issues. Incomplete personal histories lead to incorrect diagnoses. A meth addict can have true bipolar disorder apart from their addiction, or they may just mimic bipolar symptoms when they use. Either way, it is impossible to tell the difference if they are still using it.

This leads us to the other issue of giving an accurate history. Sure, addiction comes with shame that tempts someone to hide the dirty details of their lives. However, when someone is under the influence, they may not remember all of the details necessary to make an accurate diagnosis. We call this type of person a "poor historian." All that really means is that they are terrible at remembering what happened because they were too drunk to know. Here is a practical example. I could ask a wife in the middle of alcoholism how many times per day she drinks. She may say three times with full confidence. Her husband will then turn around and say that it is at least five times per day. I could then ask her how many times per week they fight, and she will reply twice. The husband will then react with shock and say they fight daily.

With this limited information and a short amount of time to make a diagnosis, many addicts come away with a label that does not fit them. They get one that sort of explains their behavior but fails to make sense of who they are as a person. Diagnoses that describe behavior but miss the cause lead to labels that can encourage prejudicial treatment and misappropriation of time and resources. These labels also follow an addict around for the entirety of their engagement with the medical system, causing every other provider to consider them bipolar, when they may not be at all.

Now that we understand that addiction can often mirror mental health disorders, we have to be able to make sense of what is truly a mental health disorder before, in the middle of, and after active addiction. Before we can make that distinction, we have to get out of the chicken or egg argument from earlier. There is no way to tell if someone has a true mental health disorder in the middle of active addiction. What we can do is look at common mental health disorders that exist in active addiction and see how they line up.

We can start with anxiety. As an integral part of the human experience, anxiety is something that is both necessary and possibly concerning. No one's goal should ever be to rid themselves of all anxiety. Without some concern, we are unsafe. And without stress, we are unable to find courage and development. We all know what anxiety feels like to some degree. Some theories guess addiction is the attempt to reduce anxiety, to cope with stress. Those that have experienced addiction also know that anxiety exists in the middle of it and even after. Part of this is normal. If we think about the last chapter on Attachment Theory, there is certainly some element of anxiety regulation in connection to a substance. More than just anxiety reduction, substances represent safety, and the ability to make sense of the world. Just as the breakup of a romantic relationship brings anxiety, so does a disconnection from the drug that makes the world quiet again.

In the middle of active addiction, anxiety can become relevant with intoxication and in-between times of use. Stimulants, also called uppers, can engage the stress-response part of the brain, making someone paranoid or on edge. For those in severe addiction, this anxiety leads to obvious outward signs, such as rapid speech, paranoia, and distrust of others. There can also be a rush of anxiety in the later parts of intoxication when the drug or alcohol starts to lose its effect. When an addict is looking at the prospect of going back to life without having a chemical buffer, great stress can come. Between the times of use, addiction can bring anxiety in the fear of needing the next dose or drink. Addicts know that withdrawal symptoms will come and give them the "flu" or whatever other term they use. There can also be an increase in anxiety with the realization of what they have given up and what they have become in the process of sacrificing due to their addiction. Surely, anxiety is present when a mother recognizes that the foster system has her children, and she is continuing to not follow the plan to get them back. When the husband becomes somewhat sober and understands that he is slowly moving farther away from his wife with each binge, anxiety begins to hit him again.

Many addicts fear overwhelming anxiety in early recovery. It can seem daunting at times. Not only are they sober enough to actually see the damage they have caused, but they do not have the same ability to deal with those emotions. To some point, it is good that anxiety floods an addict in early recovery. Like the rush of cold water at the beginning of a shower, intense feelings of fear and guilt are necessary to re-engage in the world after a lengthy emotional absence. These feelings can increase and decrease over time. However, it is important to know that anxiety in early recovery may not be all that great. It is just the addict's ability to process and tamper feelings that are lacking. In short, anxiety is normal and doable, but you just need to build an ability to deal with it that was lost in the middle of active addiction.

The treatment of anxiety in an addict should not have a goal of anxiety reduction, but anxiety adaptation. If someone in early recovery were to receive anxiety medication that removes all of the tension that they feel about the damage they have caused in relationships, then not only is the addict unable to truly see everything that they need to deal with, but they do not feel as pressured to engage, and loved ones lose their influence. If an addict becomes numbed after entering recovery, loved ones never get a voice and the addict never gets to embrace life as it was meant to be lived. While anxiety should not completely paralyze an addict, it should also not be avoided or seen as an adversary.

Depression is another great point of contention in the recovery world. Many feel depressed before their addiction, in the middle of it, and after entering recovery. Another important part of the human experience, depression signals a great loss of a relationship. It is necessary for grief and the realization that life is temporary. Some addicts will use substances to deal with depression, but some clarification is needed. Individuals do not enter the process of addiction to deal with depression symptoms. They do it to cope with what led to depression and how it affects them. Do not become overtly behavioral here.

Treating depression, especially in addiction, can easily become symptom-focused. Without feelings of depression, someone may be able to live a new life, right? Wrong. When someone with depression is relieved from their symptoms through strife and love, they learn about a new part of themselves, that life is worth living. While it is not popular to say in today's social climate, it is incredibly healthy to be depressed at times. Within the correct context, mourning and engagement with the depths of emotion help us engage with the larger questions in life. Free from distraction and able to focus on the finality in life, many have used depression to seek out their purpose in life. A great example of this is Viktor Frankl, who found meaning not in the great exhilaration of great experience and company, but in the depths of despair. In the times when life seemed to have no meaning and he was awaiting his execution, Viktor Frankl was able to tap into his understanding of what makes life worth living. Much along this same vein, I do not consider any one emotional experience to be inherently negative or positive. What we do with those feelings can determine value, but experience in itself is what makes us human.

In the middle of addiction, depression can set in for a few different reasons. Some substances have a depressing effect on the body. Alcohol is a great example of this. If there is an addict who already had depression and begins to engage in alcoholism, then the effects of drinking will lower bodily responses and resulting energy levels. Of course, someone is going to feel depressed if their body is constantly drained of energy. Depression can also set in for much the same reasons that anxiety does, the recognition of the damage that has been and is continuing to be caused. For some reason, some individuals tend towards anxiety in these in-between times, and others tend towards depression. Whatever that reason is, depression can truly cripple someone's ability to complete daily tasks, even more so when addiction has become an hourly task.

Once true sobriety hits and the addict starts towards recovery, many describe feelings of depression. While I sympathize with that feeling, I think that there is a significant part missing in this explanation. Depression is a symptom, but it is not the real problem. What is truly underneath these feelings is shame and a lack of hope. Sure, depression is a great descriptor, but it truly misses the point. Symptoms are important to manage through therapy, relationships, and possible medication. True despair of the human spirit is more than just markers of symptomatology. Much of this describes addicts in early recovery. Addicts and their families should embrace some measure of depression. Many things have been lost and thrown to the wayside over time. A period of mourning is warranted if a next step is to be considered.

Mood disorders are another category of mental health disorder that are often misunderstood in addiction. Calling someone bipolar because of mood swings is a common thing but is clinically inaccurate. True mood disorders are consistent over time and are not isolated to one event. True mood disorders before addiction exist without any precursors. One day someone could feel as if they could run three marathons in a day and the other, they feel as if they cannot peel themselves off the bed. They can be triggered by life events but are not exclusive to them.

The highs and lows of mood disorders, particularly bipolar, can easily be seen through symptoms that addicts show in their cycle of use. For the stimulants, mood swings are obvious. Methamphetamine addicts can stay up for days on end, only to crash for days after. Cocaine addicts will engage in risky behavior and become promiscuous. For substances with a more depressant effect, the lower areas of a mood disorder can be mirrored. Seeing someone constantly in a "funk" because of their use of benzodiazepines, only to get bursts of energy when shame sets in, can also seem like a mood disorder.

When looking at the difference between a mood disorder and the emotional results of sobriety thrust upon someone, there must be a great amount of clarity and accurate history present. Context is key here. What can seem cloudy before and during addiction can even seem hazy once someone enters recovery. Would a mood disorder diagnosis be relevant if someone is sleeping in every day for two weeks and then has a huge burst of energy for a couple of days, becoming hyper-productive? What if they were racked with shame and were just told that their family would kick them out if they did not contribute? So, which is it, a mood disorder, or a rush of anxious guilt to not get put out on the street? Typically, addicts in active recovery will find a middle ground of functioning that is not concerning to their loved ones. However, context and relationships are key for diagnosing a mood disorder, even in recovery.

The next category that gets constantly intertwined with addiction is psychotic disorders. These are the ones where people see, hear, and experience things that are not real. Like all the other types of disorders mentioned, there are certainly those that have some sort of psychosis that also experience addiction. However, many of those in addiction experience sensations that are a result of using substances. Something has been developing in the past few years in research worth mentioning here. Many addicts and their families wonder if the psychosis they experience in addiction will carry over into recovery. Some will. While the majority of psychotic episodes are isolated to active use, others can experience psychosis in periods of withdrawal and even after all symptoms should have subsided. It is impossible to predict who will experience long-term psychosis brought on by substance or alcohol use, but it is important to know that there are emerging cases of people experiencing long-term issues with psychosis after using marijuana. There is some guess that this is related to an underlying condition that has not come to the surface. This can be for an addict of any age. Still, there is a very real possibility of a teenager experiencing long-term psychosis symptoms after smoking weed, let alone anything else they could get their hands on.

Psychosis is one of the more frightening symptoms to experience in addiction. Those that experienced it before addiction can feel as if substances can "make the voices go away," even if that is just for a short time. Individuals that have never experienced psychosis before seem to not stop their use after an episode, chalking it up to a bad trip or something that is doable with practice. This area of treatment in long-term addiction is one of the more difficult to work with. On top of everything else that comes with recovery, there can be random voices and ideas that pop up. It is hard enough to argue with an addict about the benefits of sobriety, let alone other voices that cannot be disputed. With some truth and a knowledgeable psychiatrist, there can be healing for this too.

The last category of diagnoses I will talk about here is personality disorders. There are those with true personality disorders that find themselves in addiction, but many addicts are accused of having a personality disorder when they do not. If you have never heard of what a true personality disorder is, this book is not a handbook on what they are and how to treat them. Genuine personality disorders are much out of my expertise. A helpful way to understand them is to picture a list of emotional skills that someone has. Then, those with personality disorders heavily play on certain ones, without regard for the others. Individuals with a personality disorder struggle with social interactions on a fundamental level. It is not a simple issue of training skills; there is more to it than that.

In addiction, many accusations of personality disorders come up. If I had a dollar for every time a significant other or family member accused an addict of being a narcissist or borderline, I would be able to buy an extra collection of high-end guitars to revel in. In some ways, these loved ones are correct. Those in active addiction do show some similarities to those with true personality disorders. They can lack empathy, become highly manipulative, sabotage, and leverage relationships, and seem without remorse in the feeding of their addiction. Personality disorder labels have been used to club addicts into better behavior. As was mentioned earlier, just because someone can fit criteria does not mean that they truly fit that diagnosis. I will say that a particularly skilled licensed clinician is needed to spot and treat personality disorders. Even if I felt entirely comfortable working with personality disorders, I would not dream of working with them if they are in active addiction. So please, stop calling them narcissistic. They are selfish and short-sighted. Call them that instead.

Observing Ego and Arrested Development

If you are an addict reading this section, you may get offended. If you are a loved one of an addict reading this section, you may get enlightened. No matter which end of the spectrum you find yourself on after reading this, just know something. This information does not come from a holier-than-thou place. If you can make sense of what comes, you are going to see it everywhere in addicts, both those in active addiction and even in long-term recovery.

The first of these two concepts is borrowed from relational psychology, called the observing ego. It can seem a bit daunting at first, but follow me and reread if necessary. Here is the basis of what an observing ego is. Think of it as a floating eye above a person. This eye perceives what is happening to the person and what is happening around them. It takes in information and makes sense of social and emotional interactions. This floating eye also tells the person about the way they interact and the ways they are affecting others. Observing ego is incredibly important for something often found missing in addicts—empathy. Without the ability to see outside of yourself, there is no conception of what is happening to others and how your actions are affecting them. Even if there is some mechanical understanding of how your actions impact others, without an active observing ego, addicts do not feel the same emotional pull in the consequences of their actions.

This floating eye is integral for any empathetic and connected relationship. Seeing another person's perspective allows for flexibility and adaptation in response. Observing ego engages in the throes of the human experience, understanding that life and people are complicated. A healthy observing ego will see that the widowed mother has value and deserves support. Without observing ego, this woman is a drain on resources and should be ignored. A healthy observing ego will see that orphaned children need continual guidance. Without observing ego, they are a nuisance that should stay out of the way. To some extent, modern society has lost its engagement with observing ego, becoming callused to the plight of our neighbor. For the addict in active use, this extends to nearly everyone they interact with. Sure, some empathy exists for the ones they care about, but there is no long-term engagement in it. The empathy of an active addict only exists for the immediate moment. After that, it is cast to the side for drugs or alcohol.

Another important issue that arises when the observational ego is lost is the inability to experience how addiction impacts those around them. For some, they shield their emotions from the chaos of their addiction. For others, there is a total disconnection from the emotional impact that they continue to cause. It is not that they are guarding themselves against feelings but that they seem to not perceive it at all. This can be incredibly frustrating for families who want to shake their addicted loved one, hoping to get them to see just how bad things have gotten. To the loved one reading this, relieve yourself of the need to show them just how badly everything has gotten and how much they have hurt everyone. They likely cannot recognize it right now. Later, once they have gotten their skills and emotions back, you can rip into them about how their actions affected everyone. Obviously, in a healthy context, this is needed for your healing and the development or re-engagement of your sense of empathy. If you are reading this and they are still drinking or using, now is not the time. If they are in recovery, the opportunity is there, but it needs to be set up properly.

So how do we get that floating eye working again? It may seem as if addicts have lost all sense of themselves and cannot feel empathy for others. I will give you something in an analogy that can be helpful. Going with the eye thing, imagine you have had your eyes closed all night from sleeping. Then, someone flips the lights on. This is what addicts are faced with in early recovery. This inhibited observing ego now has to make sense of a great amount of input. It will feel blinding, like they want to close their eyes again. Too bad. It's morning and time to wake up. Many family members want to then push into the addict and scream about the destruction that addiction has left. For that, we will consider those blinding lights the doctors flash to test the responsiveness of your eyes. If you wake someone up from a night's sleep and immediately shove that wretched thing into their eyes, you will not get much of a different or satisfactory response. Let their eyes settle again, and then hit them with reality after new information can be taken in.

From this concept, understand that addicts are not completely inept and incapable of empathy. Their eyes are strained and sometimes closed. They can open back up in active recovery. Without re-engagement in substances, most have the opportunity to start seeing again, engaging in observing ego. They can truly perceive the end result of their addiction and begin to give genuine support and repentance for what has taken place.

The second part of this section is definitely a crowd favorite. Any time I would teach about this in treatment, addicts would start seeing themselves in a different light and start using the information on their peers. Explaining to supervisors about calling my caseload children and their peers the same was always fun. Arrested Development is not a new concept. It started with a brilliant psychologist named Erik Erikson. He theorized that everyone goes through stages of development that follow one another in order. Erikson gave specific goals for each stage that correspond with specific age ranges. Over time, these stages would lead to lessons that would build on one another. The idea was that if someone was unable to resolve a stage, they were unable to resolve any of the other stages as well. They would be stuck on a stage until they could resolve and move on. They would continue to fail at the other ones as well.

Here is the overview of the stages. There is some wiggle room for age ranges, but not much. Birth to 18 months represents the task of Trust vs. Mistrust. This stage hopes to learn if the world can be trusted, if hope can be found. Mostly through parents, these children ask for their needs with the expectation that they will be met. If this goal is not met, children do not trust anyone or anything and are likely to psychologically insulate themselves. The next stage is Autonomy vs. Shame which takes place from 18 months to three years. In this, children figure out how much will they can impose on the world. These kids need to learn that their voice means something. If they fail at this stage, children lose an individual voice and will. The result is an individual that cannot make sense of who they are. After that comes Initiative vs. Guilt for ages three to five years old. In this stage, children learn that they can impose their will with a purpose. If they are not able to meet the needs of this stage, they are unable to make decisions and become paralyzed in any attempt to move forward. At five to 13 years old, children engage in the task of Industry vs. Inferiority, hoping to find competency. Somewhat related to confidence, this stage requires that children learn that they can show skill and involvement in the world around them. If this is not met, then children struggle to believe that they can make good decisions. Shame can come upon them and make it difficult to make rational decisions. Then, the task of Identity vs. Role Confusion comes. At ages 13–21, individuals find their separate personalities and fidelity in their identity. You often find individuals trying on different "hats" to see what identity and social group fits them most comfortably. If they fail in this stage, people struggle to see themselves as a steadfast individual and become overly attached to others. Then, individuals move to Intimacy vs. Isolation at ages 21–39. Here, people hope to find love and true connection. When someone is not able to meet this task, individuals are unable to make intimate and vulnerable connections with others. After that, Generativity vs. Stagnation stands in front of people from the ages of 40 to 65. Here, there is a turning point with a focus on caring for those that come after them. If there is a failure here, then no positive impact is made on those after, leaving little motivation for others to speak kindly of them. Finally at age 65 and older, comes the task of Integrity vs. Despair. Here, individuals are given the opportunity for wisdom. If they fail at this, individuals will feel as if their life was wasted.

Now that we have this list of goals in front of us, we can see how someone can start to struggle. For instance, if someone is not able to resolve the task of Industry vs. Inferiority, they will then lack competency, fidelity, love, care, and wisdom. If they fail in Initiative vs. Guilt, they will lack purpose, competency, fidelity, love, care, and wisdom. Along with this failure comes obvious signs. Here is how you can see just how emotionally old someone is. When they become emotionally stressed, how old do they sound? A 30-year-old may not throw a literal temper tantrum, although that is certainly possible. They may flail and say that they have no idea how to make decisions and struggle to decide how to even proceed with treatment. That would make them emotionally around ten years old. They may not be that way in their normal routine, but these points of particular frustration show how far someone has come.

In treatment, it is rare to see anyone emotionally past their teenage years. How do I know this? Get a bunch of addicts together in treatment and see how they act. It is shocking how reactive, petty, and emotional they get. It is almost like a middle or high school locker room full of grown men and women. You can see impulsive behavior that does not grasp long-term consequences and will see their emotional experience taken as truth. Teenagers and addicts are incredibly selfish and lack an understanding of risk and possible damage due to their behavior. Because of this, family members, and particularly significant others, can see their addicted loved one as a middle-aged teenage alcoholic. Significant others will describe being in a relationship with them as raising another child. Wives and husbands feel as if they must manage great emotional swings, much like a pubescent teenager.

I said that almost everyone in active addiction has stopped growing at a teenage level or earlier. The reasons for this are vast, and we will be discussing those in the next chapter. Also, just because they have not completed Identity vs. Role Confusion does not mean that was their highest level of emotional growth. Even outside of addiction, some adults have the emotional maturity of a five-year-old. How do we know this? Have you ever heard of or seen someone get physically violent because someone was disrespectful to them? With this framework in mind, it is kind of hilarious and sad to watch. Do you mean to tell me that someone called you a bad name and now you have to throw a tantrum and hit them? Wow, that sounds like a small child getting his feelings hurt. If you have not caught the drift yet, this emotional immaturity is prevalent outside of addiction as well, but it is present in nearly all addiction cases.

When the addictive substance is taken away, the one thing that soothed the sadness and sorrow has been taken away, leaving addicts with no emotional skills and only their last successful phase of emotional development. When someone finds themselves in this position, they are thrust into the emotional skills of a child with the responsibilities of an adult. Imagine this same scenario with an actual child or teenager. It would be overwhelming. This is not an excuse for this level of emotional skill, but it is important to understand if effective treatment is to be given.

Effective intervention on arrested development is rather funny. Once the addict can be identified within an emotional age range, you can speak to them in a way that would make sense to that age. I am not insinuating that you should be demeaning to someone in early recovery. Certainly, I am not going to use baby-talk to a grown man. However, effective communication for that emotional age works like magic. I use this all the time in my own private practice. Once the intake and a few sessions have gone by, I start orienting language, speech patterns, and even body language to match a client's needs. With a 35-year-old man with the emotional maturity of an eight-year-old, we will talk about creating a new life, making people proud, and acknowledging their accomplishments. For the emotional 15-year-old, we talk about friendships and the meanings of social interactions, with a focus on how life can play out long-term. To my clients that are possibly reading this book, you may have an aha moment. Truth is, I do this with everyone in my practice. It is a ton of fun, and I see amazing engagement from it. I also use this to evaluate a client's progress. With support in emotional growth, clients will find themselves speaking and acting older over time. To the loved one reading this, do not talk down to the addict in your life, but recognize and engage in language that is appropriate for their emotional age. You will find more success with the framework and next steps relevant to their developmental phase and task that needs to be accomplished than you will working with higher emotional skills. Do not baby them, but understand that what they can hear at the time is what is most effective.

The last thing I will say here is that just because someone is 25 years behind in emotional development does not mean that it will take 25 years of work to catch up. With continued effort and support from the people around them, addicts can grow up rather quickly. To a greater point, some individuals seem to reach past their emotional stage into later ones. Some 35-year-olds consider what impact their actions will have on the world and some 17-year-olds seek intimate and vulnerable relationships with others. We call these people wise beyond their years. Addicts can reach emotional maturity. Sadly, many are left in much the same place that they left, with less drug and alcohol use. That makes them sober, but insufferable. The common term for them is a dry drunk. To the addict reading this, you can and should grow up, for your sake and those around you. Life is much more fulfilling and worth living on the other side.

CHALLENGES AND BOXES

Dealing with mental health is confusing and challenging. Adding addiction into the mix can make things much more complicated. To help separate some of these things, there are a couple of skills that I tell my clients so that they can feel more equipped and less overwhelmed. If kept in context, these things can be helpful for addiction and even other mental health disorders. Be forewarned, there is compassion and challenge in these things. There is no point in this process where care is lost, but I refuse to treat any of my clients as incapable of a healthy and vulnerable life. I do not hold a prejudice of low expectations for addicts and would rather come off as a jerk that cares enough to say the hard things than a kind one who never calls them to be everything they can be. That goes for everyone who steps into my office and will not change.

The first concept to make sense of mental health is the difference between having a disorder and being a disorder. This seems like semantics at first, but let me explain. Most people talk about things that happen to them that affect them. They may say things like "I had a headache" or "My stomach hurt." In this, they mean that something was done to them that was outside of their will and identity. This point of view sees individuality apart from outside forces, making it possible to influence what is happening around them. If someone gets a headache, it can be treated as a symptom. If someone's stomach hurts, then they can be evaluated and treated for hunger to appendicitis.

This seems rather straightforward for the majority of the population. With significant mental health disorders, the line between what happens to someone and the problematic thing being an aspect of the person is blurred. An individual with mental health concerns may not say that they are experiencing depression, but that they are depressed. The language is subtle, but there is a great difference in meaning. If a disorder is an aspect of their being, changing emotional responses is a task in identity, not symptom management. They may say something like "I am depressed," or "That's because I am bipolar." There is an enmeshment in sickness that has become so ingrained that mentally ill individuals cannot see hope for the future because that is who they truly are. Their symptomatology has become who they see themselves as.

There are many reasons why people do this. Many have not been able to see anything other than their symptoms. For as long as they can remember, they have been anxious or depressed. There is not a point in their lives that they did not feel defunct in some way. Some remembered parents and loved ones telling them that something was wrong with them and then absorbed that comment into their being. Others have felt symptoms so intensely that it can be hard to convince them that anything could change. So, acceptance is the only thing that makes sense of what is happening to them. This can become incredibly difficult to treat as a clinician. Some do not realize that asking their clients to work on their depression or anxiety can be a greater task than just practicing breathing techniques or going outside and sniffing flowers. Clients may become so intertwined with their sickness, that it defines them, and gives them a sick Secure Base to understand the rest of their lives. These tend to be some of the more difficult to treat. Their disorders are not a scrape on the skin, but a deep infection that sickens the rest of the body.

In addiction, particularly the more severe forms of it, not only is there an infection in the body, but a cancer. Addicts do not see themselves as someone who needs quick surgery and some antibiotics. Many believe that they are terminal, with no hope for recovery. Let me be clear. I do not believe that addiction is a medical disease, but something that has become so ingrained in the mind and soul of someone, that it affects everything about them. Some addicts will argue that addiction is separate from them and that they can get better if they try. This is a bid for lesser consequences and distance from responsibility. Many will even make great proclamations of their potential for change, making small changes for only a time. Still, once the intensity has worn off and they sit in silence, the feeling of a cursed identity becomes overwhelming. If addicts were honest, they feel as if addiction has become so wrapped in their souls that they are unable to tell who they are anymore.

Many practitioners have attempted to convince addicts that their addiction is outside of them, and others have said that it is not their fault. Both are wrong. Addiction is not a set of particular symptoms. It is also not something that happens without the will of an individual. Addiction is something that has slowly eaten someone away over time. Sure, they were not addicted to alcohol when they were a teenager, but they did sacrifice relationships for their own selfish desires. Retirement did not bring on addiction, but decades of distraction from their soul and relationships with others did. Addiction is not special, but the result of years of unresolved pain and self-centered ambition. That may sound harsh. It is, and I mean every word of it. Sure, the twenty-something had no intention of ruining their marriage, but drinking to distract from responsibilities and avoid loneliness set the stage and wrote the lines of a wretched play. A child is not to blame for the terrible things that happened to them, but they are responsible for how they handle it as they get older. Unfortunate circumstances and complicated relationships are not to blame for addiction. They are precursors but do not hold the responsibility of a DUI or overdose.

If you paid attention to the header of this section, you saw that I present addicts with challenges. This is not to demean or belittle anyone. It is just the truth. You cannot heal without knowing and accepting the truth. Even if you think you do, others get a route for healing as well. How incredibly short-sighted and selfish it is to blame addiction on a disease and tell loved ones that they should just accept what happened because someone was "sick." So many families and significant others are robbed of the opportunity to work on their own pain because a recovering addict was told it was not their fault. That is absolute garbage. Addicts are responsible for their past actions and future work. If we do not present them with the ability to recognize their power in a decision, then we also cripple them in recovery efforts. Without engagement in the pain and decisions that someone caused, addicts must simply wait for it all to fall apart again. Isn't that how a disease works? You just wait for it to come back, and everyone else has to deal with it.

Now that we have a proper understanding that work can be done, I will give you something that I use with all my clients with and without addiction. I call it boxing our mental health issues. Here is how it works. There are three general boxes of issues that people deal with. There is some overlap, but for the most part, it can be helpful to starkly sort out issues. Once someone's concerns are placed in respective boxes, then effective treatment can occur. We can separate what is individual to work on and what may be an outside factor.

The first box holds things that would stress out the majority of the population, called the normal box. This box can contain anything from an economy collapsing or a fender-bender. No matter who you are, those things are going to increase someone's blood pressure. In any typically functioning individual, the first box would make sense. I like to introduce this box at the beginning to normalize the life that we all live. Everyone can relate to someone close to them dying or losing a job. For this box of concerns, much of the therapeutic work is around understanding and acceptance.

These circumstances cannot be changed. Instead of pushing to re-evaluate mental health reactions, the first box is simply something to recognize and let be.

The second box holds stressors that are present due to mental health disorders or traumatic experiences, called the mental health and trauma symptoms box. This gets a little more complicated but will make sense in light of everything we have talked about. If someone is diagnosed with depression, they are going to have low energy. What they do with that goes in another box. However, the low emotional experience of depression correctly sits in this box. If someone has a legitimate diagnosis of ADHD, they are likely to get distracted often and speak over others. These are symptoms of a disorder, not any deeper concern of individual identity. For trauma, some points are reminders of past negative experiences. For instance, I have heard clients who come from unsafe neighborhoods express that screeching tires could mean danger is on the way. That may not mean anything to the general population, but to them, it is something important. Other clients have shared that when their father got home, that meant that drinking would occur and yelling would start soon after. So, they become accustomed to experiencing stress when a door is opened rapidly. Again, that type of experience is not meaningful to the general population. This second box holds most of where behavioral therapies and medication find great benefit. Giving someone with true ADHD medication almost instantly changes their ability to function. Developing skills to deal with gaps in short-term memory further develops growth. Working through sudden triggers through gradual desensitization can work wonders.

This box of mental health disorders and trauma often can be a volume knob for the other two boxes. Earlier, I mentioned my love for guitar. If you are not familiar, one thing common with us guitarists is that we look for a breaking point in an amplifier. If you shift that volume knob, things get louder. When you turn it up loud enough, an amplifier begins to "break up" the sound and create distortion. Mental health disorders and trauma can create much of the same effect. They can amplify certain sounds in the room. Then, at a point that is specific for each amplifier, things become distorted, and meanings change. To treat this aspect of mental health and addiction, volume can be lowered over time. This is one part of treatment that takes patience and continual work.

The third and final box of mental health disorders and addiction is the individual box. These are things that only make sense to the person. This box also holds specific beliefs and worldviews that affect everything else in someone's experience. While it can be reciprocally influenced by the mental health and trauma box, this one holds most of the individual work in therapy. From here, people find their perceptions of mental health and trauma. Borrowing from the previous chapter, the individual box carries the information from a Secure Base, making sense of the rest of the world. Different contents in this box allow for different responses to similar events. Sometimes, siblings can have very different responses to the same traumatic event. One will engage in healthy coping skills and relationships and the other will veer off into addiction and risky behavior. The difference, also called resilience, is found in the individual box. Resilience is what someone believes about themselves and the world, as well as how equipped they are to handle it.

Most addicts try to reject or distract from this box. This is not necessarily because they are unable to deal with it, but it may be due to the intimidating prospect of seeing what is inside. Underneath layers of addiction, unhealthy coping skills, and pain lies what someone believes about themselves. If you are an addict reading this or care about someone who is an addict, know that this box says everything about someone. The addict's individual box is full of terrible and hateful beliefs about themselves and their future. Much of addiction is dealing with the consequences of this box. After accepting the box of normal responses and managing the box of mental health and trauma, comes the intense work of examining the individual and seeing what is left. Addicts have a tendency of taping over this box and burying it in the ground, hoping to put it far away enough to drown out the voices of shame and doubt that come from it. True recovery is unearthing it and sifting through what is inside. This is where the long-term individual treatment comes from, where the soul of a healthy person can speak to the hurting addict.

Now comes the cool part of this boxing strategy. When someone with a mental health disorder or addiction feels as if something is overwhelming, it is beneficial to sort out thoughts and feelings in each box and see what can be done. That way, interventions can be specific to each part and addicts can separate their emotions and cravings from their own identities. Let's take a desire to relapse, for example, and see how this all shakes out.

For the normal box, it would make sense for anyone that has been addicted to drugs for a significant period of time to want them again. It is also very normal to want to go back to coping skills that we used in the past. Also, it makes sense to want to run away when guilt and shame are seemingly heaped upon you. If family or loved ones have left due to addiction, it makes sense to still need comfort in life. Attachment Theory tells us that wanting to feel safe and connected is an important part of life. These connections are what make life worth living. The lack of them would make anyone feel desperate. To treat these feelings, an addict should engage in conversation about what seems reasonable to be stressed about and learn to accept that life is not what they expected it to be and that they have hurt many people. Because of this pain, it is rational to want to distance yourself from what has happened. Here, explanation and time to sit are appropriate responses.

For the mental health and trauma box, many symptoms are typical for recovery. Increased anxiety and depression are to be expected. Feeling overwhelmed and sensitive is a part of the treatment process. Desires to relapse often do not come from simple stress, but a learned response that was built over time. From that, patterns of behavior are born. These patterns need to be interrupted and examined so that they can be broken. Others experience reminders of trauma after being sober for long enough. Addiction clouds thinking and judgment. Some even push memories deep into themselves in the middle of their use. Memories and trauma can easily surface once the brain can process them. Panic and a rush of adrenaline can then come into the recovering addict's brain. This is typical of the recovery process. To deal with these symptoms, sometimes medication is needed for a short time. This should only be to slow things down enough to allow for processing to take place. Compassion and guidance are key in working with this box. I often speak of this box as the weeds that hide deeper issues. Some can see this box and think that if symptoms are dealt with, then healing has truly come. While this is not the case, it is a start.

Our last stop for therapeutic work is the individual box. Of all the boxes to work with, this one provides the greatest resistance. Within this box, there are years of work that are needed. Not all of those have to be in a therapy office, but all of them require intentional work. The other two boxes require understanding and acceptance. Individual boxes do as well, but they need something greater. Once I realize that I am walking around in this box with a client, I become more reverent in the discussion. Reverence here does not mean that I do not challenge, but it does mean that I am more deliberate about wording and engagement. In this box, many find a small girl wanting to be heard, or a boy who was scared to be hurt again. Inside can also lie pains and scars on someone's understanding of their being. In an almost spiritual sense, this box contains the make-up of a person, for better or worse. After everything else is swept away, understanding has come and symptoms are managed, an addict can truly see who they are and what is left. Some are encouraged and some are greatly distraught. Honest self-evaluation is needed. Therapists and loved ones should walk alongside recovering addicts as they journey through who they are. Honor the process and the ups and downs of discovery.

For my last trick with boxes, I find that clients appreciate seeing just how much goes in each box. To help clients make sense of what their stress means and where it comes from, I have them take a concern, like a desire to relapse, and decide just how much of it is in each box. After discussion and explanation of all aspects of their desire to relapse, we can decide what to do about what. So, we can go back into our hypothetical relapse and parse out how much goes in each box. We will assume that my client's name is Julie.

Julie is an alcoholic who is hoping to find relief from her symptoms. She has sorted her boxes in this way. The normal box holds concern for how life will play out, fears of divorce, and a perceived need to escape. That box holds 20% of the stress that Julie is experiencing. For this, she should hear from others about their experience and see that change is possible. Life and relationships can easily shift over time. In the mental health and trauma box, there are increased symptoms of anxiety in sobriety, the anniversary of her father's death, and lack of sleep from restless nights. That box holds 30% and Julie should consider ways to lower anxiety symptoms, embrace feelings of loss, and manage a better sleep schedule through diet and breathing. The individual box holds Julie's deep-seated beliefs of being unworthy of relationship, fear of failure, and protection from weakness she has experienced. Holding the remaining 50%, the individual box represents the greatest amount of stress in the desire to relapse. She needs the comfort and support of friends, honest conversations, vulnerable connections, and therapy to rework and challenge her beliefs.

With these percentages can come some immediate relief. For Julie, her desire to relapse could be cut in half with acceptance of the realities of life and the management of her symptomatology. That overwhelming desire to run back into addiction could be crippled with work on specific concerns with thoughts and body and support in understanding the nature of her pain. With only 50% that requires long-term work, Julie's desire to relapse may not seem as terrifying. In my practice, I encourage clients to work with the individual box outside of session as much as possible. If the only work they do to better themselves is in my office, they will not get very far in the therapeutic process. However, if peering inside the individual box becomes too much to handle alone, I allow clients to slam it shut and bring it to their next session. The first two boxes can be handled outside of session, but the third can be daunting to hold at first.

If Julie could recognize just how drastically she could shift her thinking and responses with small changes, her outlook on recovery could seem much greater. In acceptance, 20% is dealt with, 30% is managed through medication and intervention, and only 50% is emotional work in the therapy office. Over time, these percentages may shift. I encourage clients to recognize these shifts and become active in changing them as necessary. If Julie feels a great desire to use substances during the holiday season but can remind herself of what she is worth and what the future can hold, then she can solely focus on managing symptoms through a tough time of year. If Julie were to ignore these symptoms, she could find herself much closer to using again than she might like. Maybe during the holidays, the normal box holds 25%, the mental health and trauma box holds 45%, and the individual box holds 30%. Guess what? The intervention can and should be different. With changes in dynamics and progress she has made, appropriate adjustments can take place. I hope that everyone reading this considers using boxes in their own life. It can help with everything we struggle with. If we are aware and honest about what we are experiencing, then we can make effective changes in our lives.

MEDICATION

Compared to the other sections in this chapter, this one will be the shortest. That is not because medications are not important. For some, they are lifesaving. I am not a psychiatrist and do not want to give directions that could be harmful. Instead, I will speak about some aspects of mental health, addiction, and medication that are important to the process of recovery. From that perspective, there is much to say.

As someone who takes medication myself, I know that there is great benefit in the right medication and dosage. I was one of those people for whom it was lifesaving. For others like me, medication can be the breakthrough needed to make any kind of progress. On the other extreme are individuals who are so heavily medicated that they barely show any emotion at all. Little phases them, but they are also unable to experience the fullness of life and miss out on opportunities to have fulfilling relationships.

When medication comes into the conversation around the treatment of a mental health disorder, there can be a myriad of responses. I have had many clients that recoil at the idea of taking a pill. Some retain fear from their addiction, not wanting to put another foreign substance in their body. Others are scared that if they were to take medication, they would lose who they are as a person. While many are concerned about a loss of their identity in medication, others are hesitant to take medication because they do not want to change. There are those who engage in a recovery lifestyle with a small route to relapse if they really want to go back again. Addicts can actually believe that medication will help them, so they avoid taking it to have something to blame later on.

Others can form an unhealthy attachment to medication with the expectation that it will be the "magic pill" they need to no longer be addicted to substances. This point of view hopes to reach some new thing that can make all of their problems go away. Others use medication as a way to manipulate their loved ones and fault a new medication regimen for their erratic behavior. Some addicts in early recovery will cling to medication so dearly that they ask to be overmedicated. With an increased dose, they would not have to feel the intense shame and regret that comes with waking up in the morning. Some do this consciously and some do it subconsciously, but both seek to find a "healthy" way to continue escaping from reality.

No matter what the motivations are, medications are only effective if someone remains sober. For most medications for mental health disorders, ingestion of illegal substances or excessive alcohol can make them ineffective. Even smoking marijuana can "turn off" the ability of the medication to help balance mental health needs. Any psychiatrist will tell you this, but it is worth repeating for those that are reading this book and are considering medication. For this reason, the effectiveness of medications should only be evaluated after someone has been sober for a while. Depending on the medication, type of substance, amount of time used, age of an addict, and many other factors, medication may only have a fighting chance starting at 90 days or even six months. It takes a significant amount of time for the body to readjust to a normal way of functioning. There is more to detoxification than just removing a substance; the brain needs time to settle as well. Again, all of this information should be taken to a mental health professional who is trained in the complex interactions of mental health disorders and substance abuse.

If medication is something that you or someone you care about is considering, I will give you some guidance that I give my clients. First, make this decision yourself. If you want to take medication out of pressure, then it will not last. As soon as the person pressuring you starts to create distance, you will not take it. Also, if you are committing to trying a new medication, you have to take it exactly as prescribed, usually daily. You cannot miss a couple of days per week of anxiety medication and then complain to your doctor that you are still anxious. Many medications need time to take effect, so do not expect that anything will happen overnight. Also, it is okay to be concerned about dosage and the types of medications that are being offered. Become knowledgeable about what you are taking, but stay away from advertisements. It is okay to disagree with your psychiatrist and ask for a different dosage, as long as you are honest about every aspect with all of your treatment providers.

Finally, my view of medication in mental health and addiction is that it should be a tool to enable, not a way to solve problems. The goal of medication should be to quiet the mind enough to have the opportunity to do work. If medication is used to remove all symptoms, then there is a risk that underlying issues could be missed, and an addict in recovery could assume that there is no need for any other work in their personal and emotional life. To give some examples, all addicts are going to be anxious once they hit sobriety. Medications are an option if they are having panic attacks, not if they are crying because they are afraid that their spouse will leave them. One of those is debilitating and removes the ability to function and the other is a very healthy response to the consequences of addiction. They can also be helpful if someone is incredibly depressed due to a chemical imbalance brought on by long-term use. This should be continually evaluated as progress comes, but there are very real, sometimes permanent effects of addiction. Those things should not be ignored.

Tying into our discussion about boxes, if 30% of an addict's stress is related to mental health symptoms, then medication should only reduce 30% of the anxiety they feel. When medication starts to creep into other boxes, triggers for relapse lie in wait. Make sure to have a continual discussion about all aspects of mental health with those that know you well and those that are knowledgeable about effective treatment. Keep symptoms in their box and issues of the heart in another. Do not see someone only as the symptoms they exhibit. Life is infinitely more complicated than that. Love and care are more than that.

UNDER HIS EYE

W HEN A CLIENT comes into my office, it is common for them to have deep questions about how they ended up the way they are. Many clients have heard purely psychodynamic approaches that can blame a psychological disorder on a parent that did not hug their child enough. Others feel as if there must have been some great trauma that they experienced that led them to where they are. Some clients will push any past event to the side and blame habits for their addiction as if smoking crack was like biting your nails. While the truth about the origins of addiction can be varied, trauma is inherent in the experience of addiction itself. This chapter will examine ways that trauma plays into the beginnings of addiction, as well as the entire experience of it. Take time to sit through some of the things you will read so that you may recognize and process thoughts and feelings that come to the surface. Honor the process and be kind to yourself.

INCLUDES MENTAL HEALTH

Trauma and mental health disorders are interconnected on many different levels. It is much more likely that someone can have a mental health disorder without trauma than it is for someone without trauma to have a mental health disorder. That is because mental health disorders are descriptors of behaviors and emotions that are outside of the normal range of experiences. Most common mental health disorders make no assumptions about how they came about, only that they exist. Two people can have nearly identical anxiety symptoms, but very different reasons for experiencing them. There are specific diagnoses that relate to trauma, such as Post-Traumatic Stress Disorder. Most people know what PTSD is and have some idea of how it affects people. So, I will not go into a long discussion about it. For our purposes, it is important to understand that PTSD is a response to specific experiences. It is incredibly complex and can take years to fully recover from. PTSD invokes a survival instinct in someone and is more than just an impulse; it is a feeling of life or death. To simply ask someone to change their response in a PTSD-related episode is a misjudgment of just how severely they are experiencing emotions.

Another complicating factor in working with mental health and trauma is that in some cases, mental health disorders can cause trauma. To give an example, an individual with Autism Spectrum Disorder will struggle with emotional connection and understanding social cues. There is nothing that this person could have done to prevent getting ASD. It is something that has found its way into neurological functions. Now, someone with a lack of social awareness and interconnection with peers may not be aware of bullying until it is much too late. Without the ability to perceive disconnection and disdain from peers, they may not realize that something terrible has happened until they are being laughed at by others. This experience would qualify as a traumatic event that was, in part, caused by a mental health disorder. Or someone with a neurological cause for anxiety could end up causing a tear in a family relationship, isolating them, and bringing great shame. Again, anxiety is not totally to blame here, but it does explain how a traumatic response came about.

We will talk in a moment about what qualifies as trauma, but it is worth noting that two people can experience something traumatic and come away with very different long-term responses. Individual levels of resilience play a role here, but it is common that while some experience severe symptoms in response to a tragedy, others seem to be able to move past significant emotions more quickly. Two sisters could be in the same backseat in a car crash with one moving towards healing and the other becoming emotionally stuck at that moment for the rest of her life. Living through something traumatic does not require that someone has severe trauma symptoms like that from PTSD. It also does not excuse someone from continuing those symptoms later in life. Much of my work in the discovery of addiction is not looking for causes of addiction, but factors that influenced someone towards the use of substances to cope. Trauma can have a great impact on someone's future functioning, even if that person is not immediately aware of it.

Trauma symptoms can also compound over time. This compounding can come from other individual events or even from the symptoms that arise from the original event. Having a second car crash or another experience with violence easily brings up new concerns. Also, severe anxiety from an original event can influence reactions that lead to greater issues. No matter which one of these routes is taken, compounding trauma leads to both more significant mental health symptoms and difficulty in treatment. From a mental health perspective, it is important that not only are the beginning events treated, but also the consequences of long-term issues. Many clients come into therapy for an initial concern that is really down the line of many concerns that have stemmed from traumatic experiences.

One of the difficulties in treating trauma and mental health disorders is how difficult trauma symptoms can be to pin down. In many cases, people can be diagnosed with a disorder that fits certain diagnostic criteria and get an effective medication regimen. We assume that is true of everyone seeking medication. In reality, trauma can masquerade as other mental health disorders and will not be detected unless someone is looking for them. A great example of this is a disruptive child in a classroom. In years past, the boy who always gets up and makes trouble in the back of the class was assumed to have ADD or ADHD. For that, he needed medication and a new school schedule. For some students, that was effective. For other students, their behavior was a result of a chaotic home-life, not a purely chemical imbalance. The boy who cannot sit still in the back may be fearful of sitting down because it reminds him of when he gets yelled at. He could also be scared that he is going to be punished at home for bad grades and is acting out at school to distract himself and avoid doing work. Another woman could be treated for a general anxiety disorder from her hypersensitivity to criticism and hyperawareness of people's facial expressions. Even in this case, trauma could be at the root, reminding her to keep herself safe by always being on guard. If she is hyperaware of the world, she may not be hurt again.

In all of these things, it is important to remember that there is no perfect fit for the diagnosis or treatment of mental health issues. Treatment of any mental health disorder can easily turn into some level of trauma treatment. Be aware as you are looking through your responses and concerns so that you do not find yourself treating symptoms rather than what is going on underneath.

What it is

The revolution of mental health advocacy and treatment has brought many revelations in treatment and awareness of issues. It has allowed many individuals and families to make sense of previously misunderstood behaviors. Surely, there are amazing breakthroughs because of the research and treatment that has come in recent decades. On the other hand, the spread of information to everyone who can read it also can make diagnoses and ideas seem less impactful than they really are. "Armchair psychologists" can take basic information about mental health and trauma, easily misinterpret it, and spread information that is not accurate. Because of this, some definitions and explanations will be given of what trauma actually is and how it works.

Clinically significant trauma is not a poor experience on a first date. It is not feeling offended by something that someone on the other side of the political aisle said. Those things can be concerning and even disruptive, but they do not qualify as true trauma. On the other end of the spectrum, many have considered that the terrible things that happened to them were merely things that everyone experienced. They believe that all parents scream at their children or daily fear for personal safety is a typical part of the human experience. Their personal experience of the world is incredibly unsafe and with a limited perspective, they do not understand that life is more about connection than chaos.

In a therapeutic setting, trauma is a significant event that surpasses a normal capacity of emotional tolerance. It is different from normal stressors in its push further than typical ups and downs of what is expected in emotional experience. These experiences vary in range and duration but are marked by their overwhelming impact on an individual. When these emotional experiences are not able to be appropriately processed and coped with, they result in clinically significant symptoms and disorders. Sometimes, trauma persists in this way due to ignorance of how to cope or refusal to address internal experiences. In other cases, traumatic experiences are so intense that individuals would not have any natural way to make sense of them. In these instances, trauma does not just overwhelm someone, but it sinks them, leading to overwhelming long-term outcomes.

Trauma can be divided into two basic categories. Many assume that traumatic events are simply that, events. However, there are other ways that trauma can enter someone's life and bring about trauma responses. The two categories of trauma I use in therapy are called "Big T" trauma and "Little t" trauma.

"Big T" traumas are specific points in time that have easily definable timelines and characteristics. These are the classic versions of trauma that everyone can point to. These are the car crashes, natural disasters, and sudden deaths. "Big T" traumas are events that most people can identify as overwhelming and problematic. The normal person can identify that a break-in or robbery is traumatic for someone and will leave a lasting impact. First noticed in World War I, PTSD can lock someone into moments in the past, making it difficult to move past emotionally and mentally. A recognizable version of the results of "Big T" trauma comes from veterans who experience night terrors. We can all see those moments as directly connected to traumatic events from combat experiences. Panic attacks can also result from traumatic events. Someone who has experienced sexual assault may become emotionally flooded when trying to engage with a loving partner. No matter what the "Big T" trauma was, it is usually easy to remember and point to as a source of tension in someone's life.

"Little t" trauma is different from its counterpart. This form of trauma comes from overall experiences from the surrounding environment. A shooting down the road is considered a "Big T" trauma, but living in an unsafe neighborhood for a significant time where that is a constant concern is a "Little t" trauma. This version of overwhelming experiences is more difficult to define and therefore can be brushed aside. When clients are asked about their history of trauma, this element is continually missed. A sinister version of "Little t" trauma can be found in family systems where anything and everything is either pushed under the rug or yelled about. For extreme versions of this family dynamic, emotional expression can only be accepted if it is large, leading to all emotions requiring significant responses to feel valid. "Little t" trauma can easily accompany "Big T" trauma as life progresses. For example, a child could be hurt or affected by a "Big T" trauma like abuse outside of the family system. Then, if a family does not engage, support, and talk about what happened, that child can learn that they are inherently broken and should shut themselves off from the world, leading to "Little t" trauma.

In therapy, most people are looking for "Big T" trauma without considering that "Little t" trauma can be present and even more devastating. That may seem odd at first to hear. How is living somewhere unsafe as bad as having someone shoot a family member? While not as impactful on the surface, "Big T" traumas give us a boogeyman to fight. These events can be pointed to and considered something to push against to find healing. The fact that "Big T" traumas are easily definable makes them more straightforward to address. "Little t" traumas differ in their hidden nature. They can wiggle their way into someone's mind and beliefs in such a sly way that they go undetected. For that reason, they can be more dangerous to someone's sense of self. An enemy across battle lines can be sized up and strategized against. The enemy in your camp catches you by surprise and you may never even know that he is there, sabotaging your every move. Individuals can come to believe that there is something wrong with their approach to life, their battle plan. "Little t" trauma can taint someone's experience so greatly that their point of view is so skewed, and they have no idea it is even taking place.

In these explanations, there is no evaluation of if "Big T" or "Little t" trauma is more impactful on someone. The amount of influence that trauma has on someone is not easily measured or predicted. Two people can experience the same traumas in events or experiences and respond differently, with little explanation outside of their own ability to connect and make sense of the world. Healthy trauma work is not a fishing expedition, looking for the one thing that could explain all of the responses that someone has followed through on. Both "Big T" and "Little t" trauma can affect someone so greatly that their course of life drastically shifts. Compassion and time are needed to make sense of these things and treat them effectively.

ADDICTION AS TRAUMA

In addiction, many individuals can look for some great thing that caused them to be the way they are. If there was something to blame, addicts can hope to either get treatment to change or push blame towards something to distract from their behavior. The connections that I will make to addiction and trauma will be both compassionate and stern. If that is not something you are looking for or you are averse to someone speaking harshly about the realities of treatment and healing from addiction, this next section may not be for you.

In some ways, trauma can be overwhelming. It will bulldoze someone's ability to ground themselves emotionally and make sense of the world. In others, trauma has become a bastion of unhealthy thoughts and beliefs, almost an idol that they make sacrifices to. Challenging their connections to trauma can seem inhumane and insensitive. However, clinging to something poisonous and corrosive will kill someone. I refuse to encourage someone to continue so that I can maintain an image of a caring person. My care for someone's growth and healing is greater than my hope to be seen as a nice therapist.

Not every addict has experienced a "Big T" trauma. Not everyone who has experienced "Big T" trauma ends up becoming an addict. Those who have experienced "Big T" trauma are more likely to become an addict later in life. Addicts are more likely than the general population to have experienced "Big T" trauma. There is no guarantee that working with an addict on recovery has to include "Big T" trauma, but it would be ignorant to not pay attention to it. These distinctions can seem trite, but they are important to make sense of some of the pain that is seen in addiction and recovery. Therapy in long-term recovery can often consist of an exploration of past events to help rationalize the journey that someone has taken. Many of those in active addiction will be reminded of terrible things that have happened to them, causing a further spiral in their use.

While not every addict has experienced "Big T" trauma before or during addiction, all of them have experienced "Little t" trauma. Period. There is not a single person who has been in addiction that has not experienced "Little t" trauma. This perspective has nothing to do with what happened before someone became an addict. Instead, the development and engagement in addiction itself qualify someone as traumatized. While someone may not qualify for a full PTSD diagnosis because of their use of drugs or alcohol, anyone who has worked with addicts in long-term recovery knows that they show similar symptoms for years after they first began their journey in sobriety.

To understand the trauma that addiction itself brings about, it is important to make sense of what someone experiences in addiction. In the first chapter, we talked about Attachment Theory and how it explains the wild dynamics and seemingly erratic behavior that comes from addicts. Addiction robs people of their ability to feel safe and connected in the world. It begins to substitute itself in place of what is really needed. From that isolation, addicts come to believe that there is nothing in the world that can truly connect and care for them. All they have left are substances. They are presented with a false choice until it kills them. Combining our understanding of what trauma is and how "Little t" trauma affects people, we can start to see how someone can become traumatized by the process of addiction.

If trauma is an experience that is so overwhelming that it is unable to be rationalized or processed, then the need to use substances fits that category. Those who have experienced addiction can recount times when they tried to keep themselves from using drugs or alcohol, only to find themselves so incredibly overwhelmed and desperate that they had no idea who they were. Just try to lock a severe addict in a detox room when they have a craving and see if they give rational and emotionally reasonable responses. With these great emotions also comes an inability to process. Tell that addict that their emotions will pass and that they are being unreasonable. Sit with them and try to ground them at the moment, and see what happens. Barring some great miracle, it is nearly impossible.

This persistent overwhelming feeling is accompanied by a chemical that can take them away from it all. No addict really thinks that heroin is their best friend in the best and worst circumstances, but they do believe that in the worst parts of their addiction, it was all they had. So, addicts begin a continual cycle of a great building of emotions with the need to resolve them. Unfortunately, and not surprisingly, drugs and alcohol do not solve anything. Instead, they make things worse and backlog emotional experience and store it away in some deep dark place. Like stuffing a Jack-in-the-Box, addiction both winds the spring to launch the jester and cranks the handle to make him jump. Over time, the spring does not get more relaxed. Instead, it becomes stronger, needing greater effort to keep it down and even less effort to make it appear again.

Consider the fear and love that some people have for roller coasters. When looking at a large one for the first time, it is easy to feel intimidated. Sure, riders are strapped down and safety precautions are in place, but hurling through the air in loops and drops presents some danger. After assessing the situation, many people decide to take the risk with the hope of some joy by the end of the ride. Some of them feel the exuberating rush of adrenaline and dopamine, and others feel the constricting cocktail of adrenaline and cortisol. One feels relief at the end, and the other swears that they will never get on another one of those metal monstrosities for as long as they live. The emotional experience of an addict can be seen here. They are the second rider in the scenario, at first hoping to see some joy from emotional experience, only to find that they felt worse than before. However, instead of getting off the ride and making a vow to never do anything like that again, they are forced back in line. Now, with enough rides on a roller coaster, they become less intimidating and scary; not so for the addict. Not only do they have to ride it over and over, but they are also unable to get out of line and can never find predictability in what they experience. So, they go on until the ride is shut down or collapses due to a great catastrophe.

When memories of past "Big T" trauma are absent, memories of the abandonment they have forced on others come to the surface. Not only do emotions come back that were stuffed over years, but reminders of their failure as a parent, partner, child, family member, or anything else causes greater strain. These thoughts alone can trigger a desire to use, to escape from the terrible ride that addicts find themselves on. Without coping skills and Safe Havens to run to, addicts are left out in the storms of life, only to find comfort in the alleyways of the human experience. The "functional" alcoholic is just barely keeping the fears at bay with liquor. When he is sober for too long, everything that was stuffed down comes to light. It is traumatic enough to experience "Little t" trauma, but even more so when you know that you are the one causing it to other people. As the addict is pushed through the line of their trauma roller coaster, they know they are moving further and further away from those they love.

Everyone responds to trauma differently, and addicts are no different. The easy way to see these responses are through the four F's. They are Fight, Flight, Freeze, and Fawn. Each responds to an outside stressor differently. They are instinctual and automatic but can be changed with effort and time. When someone decides to Fight, they push against whatever is stressing them out. This could be in argument, defiance, or even violence. When someone decides to engage in Flight, they run away from whatever is happening. These people will avoid, distract, or simply walk away from whatever is happening. Freeze is pretty straightforward; when confronted with stress, these individuals stop in their tracks. They are often described as looking like "a deer in headlights," quiet, or rigid. When someone begins to Fawn, they show their weakness as a way to distract from criticism or strain. This response often looks like self-deprecation, child-like behavior, or bodily posture that seems like they are being physically attacked.

We all have tendencies toward one of these responses. There are certainly good and bad aspects of all of them. There is use in engagement, disengagement, slowing things down, and self-reflection. None of these four F's are inherently bad, but the degree to which an addict shows them can give insight into just how greatly they are feeling emotion. Trauma also can be processed in reenactment and discussion. In a negative sense, unresolved trauma can be passed on through generations, causing the continuation of problematic responses. Addicts seem to tend towards this amongst each other in what are called "war stories." Objectively, stories of the best high or greatest get-away are ridiculous to consider in the middle of treatment. It is always a bummer to respond to a war story about drug use with a question about where their child was at the time of the event. Nothing shuts up an old memory of using together like a reminder of the day after. In treatment, these stories can seem like a relief to share. In some cases, they are. The difference between a war story and a testimony is how it ends. Does the addict regret their actions or see it as some medal to wear? If they identify with the latter, then they are reenacting trauma to write a positive story about it and ignore the consequences of their actions.

Those four F's also can be seen in how addicts use their substances. Is there a rush of anger that leads to a desire to use? That may be a Fight response. Do they use to get away from all of the emotions and failures? That may be a Flight response. Do they drink to be able to slow down and keep things from getting worse? That may be a Freeze response. Do they use opiates to shrink into a pathetic version of themselves? That may be a Fawn response. While not absolute, understanding these responses could help give insight into what underlines addiction for someone. Someone may be Fawning in their addiction because they have been hurt and need someone to take care of them for once. They could also be Fawning to finally get some engagement that they feel they have missed from childhood.

Triggers were mentioned in the previous chapter concerning mental health disorders. Trauma makes triggers more difficult. The reason for that is because trauma responses are linked to a grab for safety, and the best way to be safe is to predict what will happen next. An easy way to see this is in dogs. They do not understand reasons or motivations, but they do understand an order of repeated events. When a dog hears the word sit and then is rewarded with a treat when he follows the command, he starts to make the connection that more treats will come if he sits. Some dogs start to understand this relationship so greatly that they start sitting for everything, hoping to get another treat. Over time, they can learn other commands through repetition and reward. Then, they can attempt to fill in gaps of knowledge with what they already know. If a trained dog knows that his owner likes it when he sits, and there is a command he does not recognize, he will sit anyway.

Trauma responses are also readily apparent in dogs who are in shelters. Compared to dogs who have never been abused or abandoned, they show different responses to the same experiences.

For my dog, raising my hand in the air means that a ball has been thrown. He gets excited. For a dog in a shelter, a raised hand in the air often means getting hit comes next. The same trigger can bring very different responses that depend on experience. After some time, both dogs will look for precursors to a raised hand. My dog knows he is about to play when I say, "All right." He makes the connection from that, to a ball in hand, to the ball thrown to play. The shelter dog also starts to relate loud voices, to hands raised, to getting hit. To prepare for what will happen next, each dog will look for what happens right before something else happens.

In trauma, and particularly for addicts, this same process is happening, but to a greater degree. Instead of just one or two steps away from a traumatic experience, traumatized individuals make multiple steps in their heads to make sure that nothing bad happens again. A child may fear getting yelled at by an alcoholic father. To avoid another terrible experience, he may not only look for dad drinking, but what day of the week it is, how he walks in the door, and even how long it takes his father to come through the door from the car. Instead of waiting to get yelled at again, he looks for what happened right before and finds a way to protect himself. This explains many trauma symptoms that seem unrelated at first glance. That same child may become disruptive at school if a teacher takes too long to come back into a classroom after leaving. These trauma responses are always looking for how to keep the person safe by acting in the present.

In addiction, these trauma responses are happening constantly. Addiction has a way of increasing tension and symptoms in someone. Triggers for addicts to use may be so many steps away from a legitimate concern that what they call traumatic can seem to have no real purpose. For someone in the middle of active addiction, someone not responding quickly enough on the phone could lead to a belief that they are being ignored. That then leads to a fear of being caught in their lie. Then comes the fear of abandonment. After that comes a recognition that they may be totally alone. Finally, they would realize that their life has been wasted and they have pushed everyone away. If you are not an addict, this can all seem ridiculous. How can a missed phone call lead someone to use drugs? Logically, it does not. Without proper emotional vulnerability and support, it does. Addicts fear the creeping dread that always pursues them. Any hint that it may be catching up can cause a terminal spiral.

Now, anyone who has worked with addicts knows that they are incredibly skilled at coming up with excuses for behavior. Knowledge of trauma triggers is not an excuse to act irresponsibly. If you are trying to figure out what is happening with someone's mental health, there is a quick tool that is effective in my therapy practice. If someone blames themselves for being lazy, they usually have a legitimate mental health concern. If someone blames their mental health, they are usually legitimately lazy. Still, there is some element of truth in every sorry excuse that an addict gives for their behavior. The woman who blamed her use that day on her father's mean look has something important to share. Her desire to use may have nothing to do with her father's facial expressions, but everything to do with her own shame in making her father respond in that way. That feeling can then trail off into a very legitimate explanation for use. Even the bogus excuses that addicts give contain helpful information in recovery. When someone responds with traumatic responses, they are not as skilled or sneaky as they may think. In times of great trauma responses, addicts can give a wealth of great information about what they need to succeed.

In a further extension of traumatic responses, triggers can become so sensitive that they are linked to emotions. Feelings of withdrawal can lead to fear of sobriety. That would mean that they would have to speak to family and face everything that has fallen apart. From there, you can figure out how the chain of fears continues. It is for this reason that addicts categorically experience "Little t" trauma. They carry such a great need to escape that the entire human experience becomes too intense to handle. They live in an emotionally unsafe environment by being sober. So, they constantly have to run from emotional vulnerability, leaving them more desperate and alone. All that is left is to ride that roller coaster until it collapses.

After reading this far, hopefully an element of compassion for the daily experience of the addict has been made apparent. Now that this is understood, we are going to talk about the great injustice that is done to loved ones in the process of trauma work. Do you remember how we identified that living in an unsafe environment can contribute to trauma symptoms and long-term issues? That is now clearly seen in the addict. What about the family? Do they not get some element of concern for watching their loved one constantly walking the knife's edge of life and death? What about getting random phone calls at three in the morning? Is there no compassion for the wife who now flinches every time she gets a phone call from a number she does not recognize? It is absolutely abhorrent to cater to one part of the problem while ignoring the other. It can bring family members and loved ones to believe that their emotional experiences are insignificant or ignored. Sure, overdosing five times is traumatic. No one is arguing that. What about watching someone's life slowly slip from them five times? What about watching them jump headlong into the same thing that caused it and feeling as if there is nothing you can do? If trauma treatment is important for addicts in recovery, it is also important for the family system around them. These people show symptoms reminiscent of PTSD, including sleeplessness, hyper-awareness, high blood pressure, increased anxiety and depression, racing thoughts, and many other things because someone else refuses to change. That is unfair and needs to be called out. What's even worse is that in the middle of the traumas of active addiction, they did not even get the chance to drink or use. They had to sit through the whole thing sober.

If you are an addict reading this, I hope that this is an awakening to the reality of just how much work must be done. You have possible years of "Little t" trauma to weed out and deal with, let alone any other "Big T" traumas that came before use. Your task is vast, but it cannot be self-centered. Your loved ones deserve just as much validation and healing as you do. If you are the loved one, significant other, or family member of an addict, I hope you feel validated. It is truly a shame that you are often left in the dust of long-term trauma treatment. There are certain steps you need to take to engage effectively with someone who is entering recovery. They need time to adjust to a new life and emotional experience. Do not lose yourself in this process. You have given so much of yourself this far. Do not drop the rest of it now. To anyone else reading this, consider the entire system of family and loved ones around an addict too. They may not meet diagnostic criteria for insurance approval, but they are hurting just as much. Care for them.

At the end of this chapter on trauma, I want to say a few things. First, I am aware of just how daunting this entire process is. There is so much to unpack as the addict. You sold your soul a long time ago and have no idea who you are. Your loved ones do not know who they are either. The only reason I speak so bluntly about trauma and how to deal with it is that I cannot help but do so. What else can I do but be honest about what I have seen, what so many loved ones and family members have brought to me in tears? If anyone in this system is holding on to past trauma, big or small, there are two things that I give clients. Trauma is not defined by how significant it appears to other people, just by how significant it appears to you. Here is a question. Two men drowned. One drowned in 12 feet of water and the other in 12 inches. Which one drowned? Trauma is much like this. It does not matter the depth of the water that someone drowned in. Both men will have the same funeral. It just matters that you drowned. The other thing that I tell clients is to take time to deal with what has happened to them and because of them. It is imperative that you are honest and diligent in this life-long process. Finally, if you do not make peace with your past, it will bring violence to your present.

THANKS NANCY!

BEFOR THE UPDATE between the first edition and this one. When I first wrote this chapter, I based my writing on the many research articles that were present at the time. Since then, a few things have happened. First, the COVID-19 pandemic and shutdowns fundamentally restructured the way that we see addiction and recovery, with the evidence for changes only coming out around the time of this second edition. Unfortunately, there is now a worldwide case study available for everyone to examine. Second, many recovery pilot programs around the world have altered their stances on drug use and legalization. From Europe to the US, the legal ramifications of drugs are shifting. Third, I was able to conduct my own research on addiction and incarceration. I was able to witness both the desperation of those who have left prison, as well as the rot of the Ivory Tower. Fourth, the legality of some drugs has gotten rather wonky. What could have gotten someone a felony before is now on sale at a store down the street. Finally, more information around incarceration and addiction has come out, with an emphasis on what is missing in legal documentation.

Instead of rewriting this entire chapter to suit some desire to ascend to the level of reformed guru, I am going to make small changes throughout the chapter and give further clarification if needed. If anything, I hope that this edit gives you confidence that new information can bring a change of opinion and hope for the future.

War on Drugs

In every presidential administration, passion projects tend to be present. Sometimes, those passion projects end up being intertwined with significant legislation that stirs the heart of America. Some are great, and some are flat-out terrible. Enter the Nixon administration. Drug use became a significant topic of the public square, and everyone seemed to have an idea of how to fix it. Instead of reaching out to experts or boosting research efforts on how to deal with widespread drug use, the government decided to enact harsher penalties for the use and possession of substances. I will refrain from the minutiae of legal charges and implications, but just know that was the idea. Legislate drug use so that drug users will stop using drugs. If drugs are going to be illegal, then we have to decide which ones are more illegal than others. So, drug scheduling was born and then became tiers for which drugs were considered more harmful, potent, and easy to transport. Seems like a decent idea, right?

Nixon and his administration ended up making a huge deal about this. His "War on Drugs" is still remembered in name to this day. It has had such a significant effect, that even people who never lived during the Nixon era can even describe what it is, a total disaster. A short look into what drug schedules contain is a great first clue. The most dangerous stuff should have the most significant consequences. Well, that is only somewhat true. Schedule I drugs are the highest level. One of the drugs in this category is heroin, an evil that has ravaged many families. Alongside it is methamphetamine, a stimulant that is cheap to make and one of the most difficult drugs to become sober from. Another partner in this is marijuana. Yes, you read that right. Nestled against two of the most dangerous street drugs in our modern world is the devil's lettuce. Now, I am not a proponent of any drug use, especially when it comes off the street, but something is clearly off here. Any police officer will tell you that someone high on heroin or meth is a danger to themselves and those around them. Individuals high on marijuana are couch potatoes with slow reflexes and are a danger to Cheetos bags.

There was the boogeyman to pursue. This drug was easy to find and to blame for rotting the brains of Americans everywhere, and it was pouring in from Latin America. Not without significant risk, marijuana was akin to heroin in the public eye. If you are not aware, heroin overdoses lead to the body shutting down. Meth overdoses lead to heart attacks and strokes. Marijuana overdoses lead to being useless for a day, with a chance of psychosis if you are at a previous risk. Still, there was something to blame for all of America's woes and skyrocketing incarceration rate.

Something else to note here: legislating drug use came from a fundamental misunderstanding of human behavior. Treating antisocial behavior as criminal with the hopes that the inner motivations change is nonsensical. If, instead, the Nixon administration was hoping to lower or end drug use, it failed again due to a misunderstanding. People who use drugs are not likely to stop using them after they are incarcerated. They are likely to use them in prison and continue afterward. Nixon was barking up the wrong tree here. A hard and unforgiving approach to eliminating the importation of substances would have had a much more significant effect. Still, it is understandable to criminalize drug use for the sake of the public.

TOUGH ON CRIME

Following the astounding accomplishment of the Nixon administration came the brilliance of the Clinton administration. Instead of a simple war on a group of inanimate objects, a better idea came. We could simply just do more of what we are already doing, except we could make it worse and with more severe consequences. If at first you don't succeed, try, try again! In all honesty, there was an incredibly myopic understanding of how criminal behavior interacts with the plight of addiction. Those making legislative decisions were likely ignorant. I am invoking Hanlon's razor here, hoping it applies. To the chagrin of individuals and families for decades to come, the Tough on Crime initiative was born.

You see, criminals just did not seem to get the picture. If something is illegal, you are not supposed to do it. Arresting and charging them didn't seem to get through to them. For some incomprehensible reason, the punishment did not shift the behaviors of those who were mentally ill and addicted. I am separating these from individuals who engage in lifestyles marked by criminal behavior, taking from others and hoping to avoid consequences. From this ideology, a shift began to form in the legal system. Autonomy in sentencing and alternative methods were taken away from judges. Instead came minimum sentencing laws that required everyone convicted of a crime to serve a particular amount of time. This meant that no context or consideration was needed to give a sentence, and diversionary opportunities became nearly impossible to implement. Some diversion programs are popping up around the country as the Tough on Crime plan for reducing substance abuse has been replaced by cost-effective options.

There is yet another point to mention in this saga of cracking down on criminals. Gathering the brilliance of decades worth of knowledge in criminal justice research came the push for a Three Strikes amendment, which increased penalties when an individual was convicted of three qualifying crimes. The plan was to scare criminals from continuing illegal behavior. It worked for the general population. The level of violent crime did go down. For the addicts, something terrible happened. Those who were committing theft and petty crimes for drug money were lumped into the same criminal justice programming as those who were engaging in severe anti-social behavior, who happened to be caught due to their substance abuse. I am making a distinction here that came from my own research. It can be difficult to parse population data, but for those who are arrested and incarcerated for drug use or possession, there are two overall categories: those who commit low-level crimes for and due to drug use, and those who commit larger crimes, but are only successfully convicted of drug charges.

ACCEPTING THE REALITY

From the first to the second edition of this book, this section has replaced the text on profiting from imprisonment. There were a few reasons for this. First, as more analyses have come out, some of the arguments on private prisons have had a lesser effect than previously expected. While there are significant issues around the profiting of the prison system, it would be disingenuous to frame that as the greatest issue facing addicts and imprisonment. Instead, I have reworked this section to take a look at some of the more upsetting things I have learned through my dissertation research and review of long-term literature.

If you are considering looking into the field of addiction treatment, just know that the landscape is incredibly bleak. Not many options exist to promote warm feelings in the hearts of treatment providers or researchers. The rate of recovery is incredibly low, and opportunities for sobriety are surprisingly rare. I will do my best to go through some of the more concerning issues to shed light on where we are with addiction and incarceration. You need to know that recovery and diversion rates are low. The programs that are successful are rare and not often looked favorably upon by the government and public. What is often implemented are drug programs doomed to repeat failure and small diversion programs that can only serve so many individuals.

First, it is incredibly difficult to sort those who use drugs and commit petty crimes for money from those who live a severely antisocial lifestyle and are convicted of drug charges. When looking at criminal data through the FBI or other databases, the only information listed is what someone is convicted of, not the charges dropped, lowered, or unable to be brought. Individuals who traffic drugs, engage in gun violence, and hope to skirt the law look strikingly similar to individuals who are convicted of open use or possession, as they were taken up by a well-meaning police officer. Also, there is an argument to be made around how much criminal behavior is allowable before enforcing long-term prison sentences for the sake of the public good. Without any change and double-digit arrests within a short amount of time, even the addict who represents more of a nuisance than a threat is at real risk of removal from the public.

Another tough reality to swallow here is the bleak reality of what is currently being offered for addicts. Instead of expensive and intensive therapy programs, addicts are offered drug-replacement programs. Most often, these programs give addicts Suboxone or Methadone to curb drug use. While it was initially assumed that these FDA-approved medications could be taken for a short period of time to taper off use, it seems that sense of hope was unfounded and fuels more issues. Many doctors and advocates of these drug-replacement programs will say they are a viable treatment model, but they are often removed from the reality of these programs. What treatment is assumed to be and what it often becomes is rather different. Oftentimes, addicts sell these freely offered medications or use them to enhance their own use, adding more potent opioids or adding a different substance for a more complex high. Even programs that have attempted to remove legal consequences and add drug programming, such as was the case in Oregon, fail. The vast majority of public programs, other than drug courts with strict regulations, are attempts to stall or ignore issues.

One of the other areas people turn to as a last-ditch effort to engage in sobriety and an opportunity for change is the carceral system. The cycle of jail and prison is a rather depressing and mixed bag. With different states, wardens, and ideologies, there is no consistent environment to start to examine the effects of incarceration on drug use. What I can speak to is what I have learned through my dissertation research and long-term research. Jails seem to be more positive experiences for the common addict. For one, they only hold those who are incarcerated for less than a year or those who are in flux between intake and release. The population there seems to view their time as transient and less likely to import drugs. Prisons, on the other hand, are often full of drugs that many use daily. But just how does that happen? Easy, correctional officers are paid off to bring them in, and administrators turn away because daily intoxication is better than daily violence. The most hope I have seen and heard is Therapeutic Community programs that provide an oasis for the very few who want to see a difference in their lives.

The last issue that is important to highlight here is something that is obvious when thought about and highlighted in almost all of the interviews that I conducted. Addicts only change when they want to. Any attempt at coercion or leveraging is met with resistance. You cannot force long-term change. For those who do want to see a significant change, they are in the remarkable minority. The vast majority of addicts within the wide range of the criminal justice system do not want to change, no matter what consequences are thrown at them. If sanity were to be retained, an acceptance of inevitable failure for the majority of addicts in the criminal justice system must be accepted. If their use has not been curbed by jail and potentially prison, they have long journeyed down a road few leave.

HOPE FOR THE FUTURE

Many have tried to come up with a way to address overcrowding in the incarceration system. I will talk about what does not work first, and then we can move to what does. Some states have taken an extreme approach by releasing inmates in large numbers and hoping for the best. This is a terrible idea. There is no excuse for taking advantage of others and engaging in criminal activity that harms others. However, for those with no work history, skills, or ability to find community, what options do they have to make a way for themselves? If they have not grown or become more accomplished while incarcerated, then they only have what they were doing before they were arrested.

Other programs have opted to completely decriminalize drugs and drug use, even going so far as to provide the tools needed for the consumption of drugs and safe places to do it. This can be a decent effort, as mentioned in a previous chapter, but ultimately does not address the issue. Unfortunately, decriminalization does not leave an opening for legal private production. Instead, it means that government regulations are put into place and inspections are needed for any store that could be involved in what were once illegal substances. This switch from illegal to legal has been attempted in the US with marijuana and has created other issues. With government supervision involved, costs go up for legal dispensaries. They have to increase prices to remain profitable. So, a new black market appeared that undercuts the legal distributors, causing a lack of sales and an overall loss of power in implementation.

So, straight-out criminalizing does not work, and legalizing does not seem to work. What do we do instead? The answer is somewhat complicated but also fairly straightforward. Even the motivating factor could be agreeable to nearly everyone. Funnily enough, the answer is money. Now, I do not mean that we should throw more money at the problem. That is clearly not the solution here. What I do mean is to use the costs of imprisonment and relapse as a motivating factor. It is more expensive to keep a revolving door of incarceration for an individual than it is to attempt an effective intervention. If successful treatment is more fiscally responsible and is less hassle for police officers, then why not try it?

Let me explain what I mean by treatment. I do not mean therapy necessarily. Instead, filling in the gaps that incarceration leaves for individuals is the key. There has been much success in job and career training for those incarcerated. When former inmates leave, they can connect to a job for money freely given by a business, rather than the government. Also, studies have shown the benefit of giving a career track to inmates so that there is hope for a different kind of life. Other forms of effective treatment are drug courts. Based on a diversionary philosophy, drug courts can avoid direct incarceration and engage individuals with services as a part of their parole requirements. This accountability has led many out of sobriety simply due to the risk of failure, coupled with the benefits of continued check-ins from parole officers and therapy appointments to address problematic behaviors.

Therapy can be incredibly beneficial for helping with the

transition out of incarceration. The problem in therapy inside a correctional setting is usually due to a lack of funding and massive caseloads. Outside correctional facilities, therapy can also be difficult to engage in as attendance, payment, and effective therapists are often cited by parolees as challenges to success. There is a distinct lack of connection with the needs of addicts in the correctional system and services that can meet those needs. Another gap is the lack of training and support for therapists and mental health professionals to treat this incredibly vulnerable and sometimes volatile population.

As a result of the decades of legal precedent, any solution to this problem is not going to be easy or swift. Be cautious of anyone with a quick fix for addiction and prison populations. Before us are generations of people who have been affected by addiction and incarceration. Just as it took decades to get here, it may take decades to heal. Beyond time for healing is time for attitudes to change. Many of those in authority in correctional systems held to the Tough on Crime belief of using the correctional system as a way to lower crime and struggle with a transition into diversionary and restorative intervention.

In the meantime, for individuals with drug charges and petty crimes, support and funding for drug courts are incredibly beneficial in the long run. We know that simply locking someone up does not fix their behavior patterns, but upholding sobriety and accountability for probation is necessary. Often, drug courts still have the option of incarceration if an individual does not adhere to the requirements of their probation, thus giving an additional factor of motivation. Drug courts can also see great benefits in partnering with local treatment centers and mental health professionals as a way to outsource treatment and keep someone from time in jail, which has more severe effects.

For individuals who fail to succeed in this diversionary program, a dedicated section of a correctional facility should be offered for more intensive services. Consider drug courts as an outpatient program, and this idea as an inpatient program. Through joining with drug courts, inpatient facilities can treat inmates with unique treatment models, such as the Therapeutic Community to help bolster prosocial behavior, work on addictive patterns, and also serve the time required of them by state regulations. While these types of programs can be seen as experimental by some, there has been significant literature from programs around the country that see great progress in the treatment of addiction in their community, as well as lowered rates of recidivism.

If none of these are available to support the individual, there are budding programs that are attempting to change the experiences of those leaving jail or prison. There are programs around the US that are starting to pull government funding to bypass parole and instead create a treatment program that allows individuals to live on a campus, develop skills, and prepare for a smoother transition into the workforce and community. These are few and far between, but they seem to be the most promising alternative to simple release from jail or prison. If these programs are empirically-studied and replicable, they may prove to be one of the most effective tools in helping those who want to see a difference in their lifestyle outside of incarceration.

The last thing I will say about this is that I do not wish to abolish the prison system as a whole or pretend that there should be no consequences for affecting others through addiction and its consequences. In support of those struggling with addiction, I also have empathy for those in the community who are affected by their actions. If an addict is stealing from a store to fund their use, the store owner is affected either through loss of inventory or higher insurance rates. They deserve to have support in the reform as well. In our quest to support addicts in reintegration, we cannot forget the families who may have suffered abuse or damage to their property or sense of safety. I feel for them as well, and they deserve measured justice. We need support from the entire community in change, and this frame of thinking will be how we get it. To put it simply for those who wish to speak to others, here is something to consider. The current system is not working. There is an incredibly great cost and gaspingly low benefit to high levels of incarceration and strict penalties. While the removal of all restrictions is unreasonable, alternative methods of intervention are both cost-effective and bring less societal and financial strain on the general population. It will take time for things to change, but the support of the community will move the system towards healing.

Per Jimmy Dugan

WHEN I SPEAK about how family systems work, I imagine I seem like a conspiracy theorist or one of those guys who has a gigantic board with red twine pinned to random pictures. To my wife, I am sure that this picture is somewhat accurate. I love her to death, but I can also see her eyes glaze over when I explain these concepts in all of their complexity. I could talk about this stuff all day. Here's the short version of what I mean by family systems. They are the interactions that family members have and the relationships that are sustained over time. Aside from my own speeches about how relationships work, there is something very important here. In the realm of addiction literature, two camps rarely collaborate. These two are addiction counselors and theorists, and those with a systemic understanding of relationships. The addiction-minded folks are well-read and have invaluable experience but miss great insights into how addicts see the world and can find healing. Therapists and researchers from a systemic background do not work with addicts because they lie and make family therapy much more complicated. While I hope this is of help to the loved one and the addict themselves, the joining of addiction literature and family systems literature creates a wonderful opportunity for healing that has long been missed.

SYSTEMS THEORY

Before I get into explaining how systems impact addiction and recovery, it would be helpful to explain just what systemic theory is and where it came from. Before my field of Marriage and Family Therapy, came into existence there was a desire to search out a more holistic understanding of why people do what they do and how they could be supported in healing from these things. Without going into a full history lesson, there are some major concepts and milestones to recognize before moving forward.

The very beginning of a "Systems Theory" came from a biologist named Ludwig von Bertalanffy. His work and theory highlighted the interconnection of the world around us. There is a balance in nature that both takes from excess and gives to missing elements. No implication is made about any choice by flora or fauna, but shifts as necessary. When the balance is disrupted, the ecosystem begins to struggle and attempts to regain a stable interaction. Beyond just the interaction between organisms, the attempt to rebalance was of interest.

A great practical example of this need for balance is found in the American forest ranges. During the expansion of settlers into mountainous and forested areas west of the Atlantic coast, a significant problem arose. While man was accustomed to his position at the top of the food chain, the local wolf populations saw a threat to their safety and food supply. In response to the need for self-protection and fear of a restricted food supply, wolf populations were either driven out or pushed to extinction. With no isolated event possible in nature, something drastic happened. Local deer populations began to flourish beyond their normal limits. This may seem great at first but came with a serious issue. You see, deer are adapted to a position of prey that affects their development and reproduction. From this, deer need to birth as many offspring as possible and be able to perceive danger well enough to avoid the hunt of wolves. While wolves are predators, they are also limiters. Sick and genetically deficient deer were easily eaten and were not able to reproduce. Those without sufficient fleeing power were also eaten and unable to continue their terrible survival skills.

Now that the barriers of being preyed upon were gone, deer populations both grew in number and deformity. They also started affecting other wildlife around them, taking a food supply that was not previously needed with wolves in the picture. The overabundance of deer then led to a lower food supply for other animals in the forest. To some, the current solution is barbaric and unconscionable; to others, it is a practical and cheap way to put food on the table. Whatever your viewpoint is on the hunting and killing of deer, there is no debate about how effective well-regulated hunting has been on the sustainability of deer populations and local ecosystems. In short, responsible hunters are taking the place of displaced wolves and keeping the balance of living things in American forests.

This dynamic of needing balance and the attempt to maintain it is called homeostasis. In family systems, this can be called "keeping the peace" or "just doing what you have to do." All systems tend to find a center and will attempt to keep it. For families, this homeostasis can mean many different things. Know now and remember throughout this chapter that homeostasis is a pattern that is recognized. This balance is not inherently good or bad but simply is. A family can create a culture of openness that will push to remain open. If a family meeting is always held on Monday nights and is missed for some reason, parents or children will likely feel concerned about the flow of the rest of their week. If a mother is typically quiet to balance her boisterous husband, it will feel odd if she suddenly lays down the law and demands change from the children. Homeostasis can also foster negative interactions, which will be the focus of our addiction-minded lens. A typical example of this could be the only child who is accustomed to having each of his demands met in a timely manner. Both parents may find it easier to just do as he asks to avoid conflict. Over time, what was once an annoying habit has developed into a child that cannot handle rejection from any adult.

Just as every point in the ecosystem remains interconnected, so does every family interaction. That child who became demanding can increase his parents' stress levels, causing everything from poor work performance, to weight gain, to high blood pressure. Keep in mind that homeostasis says nothing about who is right or wrong. Instead, it just describes the interconnection of all family members and the subsequent effects they have on one another. Solutions to a spoiled child can come from every direction, some more helpful than others. You could correct the child with consequences and rewards so that they can learn about the future outcomes of their behavior. This one is quite common for short-term solutions but ultimately misses the point.

Another major milestone in the development of Systems Theory was from a facility called the Philadelphia Child Guidance Clinic. While they have decades of research and experience to boast about, one experience stood out to early systems theorists. The clinic took in adolescents who were wayward and unable to be controlled by their parents. Once admitted into the facility, these children were given significant structure and guidance. Coupled with therapy and planning, substantial support was given. Over time, defiant children were not just compliant, but even somewhat understanding of the circumstances and consequences of their actions. They had become model citizens who seemed unlikely to return to their old behavior.

When discharge finally came and the adolescents were sent back home, something strange happened. They went back into the same behaviors, almost as if they never received treatment in the first place. Somehow the training and intervention in the clinic were not enough. Like night and day, these children jumped right back into what got them into trouble in the first place. Brilliant minds came together and recognized something; the environment changed. Whether it was simply the place they were living, or something more complex, where the children were located influenced their behavior.

Over time, it became apparent that it was not simply a geographical location that determined the children's behavior. It was the family they went back to. All of the rules, expectations, consequences, relationships, and support dropped once they left the clinic. Without adherence to the new types of relationships that stabilized the adolescents in the first place, relapse into old behavior was predictable. Like the deer in our previous story, their behavior was affected by the ecosystem they were placed in. Different from the deer, it was not forests or streams that influenced behavior, but family dynamics and homeostatic interactions that thrust them back into what they were trying to escape in the first place. Put simply, the clinic was a safe place that allowed for healthy growth and support. The family dynamics they returned to did not adapt to a new type of child and pushed them back into their old roles.

A final point of importance in Systems Theory is the idea of transgenerational issues. This is how beliefs and interactions are passed down through families, parents to children. A parent's beliefs and relationship with their child will influence what a child sees in the world and what they can expect. Harkening back to our first chapter, Attachment Theory tells us that the attachments of parents and children influence emotional health. Think of transgenerational issues as the long-term consequences of those interactions. The grandfather that was harsh on the father led to the strict discipline of the son. The uncle who struggled with alcoholism leads to the mother who fears alcohol and screams at the child who innocently asks what beer tastes like.

If you have time and patience to see how your own family interacted and what effects it may have had, I encourage you to research genograms. Genograms are a graphical representation of family heritage and relationships. We can know intuitively how everyone is treated and how each person sees others in their family, but to see the intertwining of health and sickness in a multi-generational family is something to behold. These charts can be as simple or complex as you would like. You can track anything from how each member interacts with one another, to how specific mental health disorders track throughout generations.

Next, we will review how these transgenerational issues affect someone when addiction is involved. Do not take this information as only applicable to addiction. It certainly can apply to a myriad of family dynamics, whether or not anyone has a drop to drink in their lifetime. Family systems are much more alike than they are different. You may end up seeing other sober sections of your family mirroring patterns found in families involved in addiction. That is completely normal. We are all flawed to some degree. Having an open and curious mind does make all the difference.

As a Child

In these next two sections, we will explore what it is like as someone who sees another family member in the middle of active addiction. Again, none of what will be mentioned is the case in every circumstance. These are possibly present when addiction has taken hold and unhealthy patterns existed long before regular substance use became the norm. What results is mangled and marred homeostasis that keeps addiction alive.

Continuing to utilize Attachment Theory to make sense of how people grow and develop, we will take a journey through the world of a child who sees their parent live in active addiction. The mind of a child is constantly in development, learning from every interaction. The behaviors, beliefs, and relationships that are modeled for them not only give a blueprint but also a framework to understand the world around them. One thing you should know about children is that they are not dumb. They can perceive family dynamics from a distance and can feel the strain between their parents, even if it is never acknowledged. The downside to this perception is that while they can see that something may be wrong, they are ignorant of the details of what is happening. Without life experience and reflection on the way that life can develop, they make guesses from their perspective about the motivations for certain actions and beliefs of others. Children fill in the gaps the best they know how from the information they have.

When addiction comes into play for the parent, children are often left in the dark about what is happening. They will undoubtedly feel the stress from family members and the constant anxiety that surrounds their parents. Their limited perspective may only be able to see two distinct aspects. Their parent uses a substance that they have heard of, and it may be their fault. Children will often blame themselves for addiction and the faults of their parents due to their limited understanding of the world. With this model playing out and results starting to become solidified, children of addicts can come to believe that not only is the use of drugs and alcohol normal, but it is just the way that people handle things when stressed or overwhelmed. It becomes so ingrained in their thinking, that using substances could even seem like a rite of passage, a way to pass into adulthood.

Now, let us assume that a child can understand the detrimental effects of drugs and alcohol and vows to never try anything illegal in their lives. Addiction still informs their understanding of how to work with emotions and interact with others. Since children learn about the world from their parents and can only work with the information they have, they internalize an unstable emotional regulatory system. Without the skills and modeling of the healthy processing of emotions and stress between individuals, particularly their parents, children are left to guess how to handle their own emotions and relationships. They nearly inevitably fail and are left with varying degrees of emotional immaturity and a lack of vulnerable and meaningful connections with those that could support them.

Without effective intervention, children become adults much like their parents. In the most severe circumstances, the heroin-addicted father passes his vice to his child. Even if he swore that he would never allow his child to endure what he does, his lack of reform in his own life has left his child handicapped. The father's lack of humility in seeking change gave a wretched inheritance to his son. I have seen this play out in alcoholic family systems as well. It is not uncommon to hear of the alcoholic in treatment recounting family gatherings consisting of the need for alcohol. Some even share that when the family gets together, everyone has their own beer cooler, and it is expected that everyone drink or they feel unwelcome. When they have attempted to be sober at family gatherings, families may find them uncomfortable to be around and are unable to form a connection.

Going back to the experience of a child with an addicted parent, there are a few different ways that children tend to respond. Three roles emerge from these responses, creating patterns that can be tracked and interactions that can be predicted. With his prediction comes the influence of homeostasis. Once patterns are set, the family system will often enforce these rules. We will look at what these roles are, as well as how these roles can impact adult relationships with family and possible substance use themselves.

All three roles will have positive and negative effects. Know that none of these roles are inherently healthy but fulfill a purpose in dealing with stress in the family system. It is the extreme version of these roles that drives unhealthy relationships. The first child with an addicted parent is the Hero. This child's role in the family is to be a shining light in the family system. Their accomplishments and recognition are often the focus of family conversations and sacrifice. When the Hero is young, they are told about their greatness or potential for it. This greatness is guarded by the parents and given both support and correction. It is the child's purpose in life to be amazing and convince others that they are just as amazing as their parents seem to believe. They also carry the burden of having to be enough to keep their parents from fighting. Heroic children suffer from the weight of their parents' relationship and can even find themselves pushing to perform or achieve to make their parents happy enough to stop fighting all the time.

In the general population's experience, Heroic children are often revered for their ability to perform, but also for their "grown-up" sense of maturity. Hero children are easily seen in two obvious places: the ball field and the pageant stage. Not every child who plays baseball bears the burden of being good enough to make their parents' marriage stay together. If you have ever been to a child's baseball game, have you seen the parents who lose their minds and religion when a call does not go a certain way? My goodness, this is baseball for middle schoolers. None of them are going pro and still, some parents seem to base their entire life on the results of the ninth inning. In another extreme scenario, there was a pop culture phenomenon related to child pageantry. Like all good trash television, there were documentary-style episodes following children, some of them still in diapers, and their parents through beauty pageants around the country. If you can get through the thousands of DCS reports that could have been filed, some parents swore that their child was the best at everything. They would even spend thousands of dollars on a dress for a single pageant with a $500 prize. It was almost foreign to the parents that their five-year-old smiling and walking awkwardly around the stage was just uncomfortable and off-putting, especially when parents were bombastically screaming at how amazing they were.

At some point, Hero children start to buckle under the pressure that their parents place on them. Children are not dumb, but they are ignorant. When they see that their parents are not happy and constantly fighting, but seem better when they perform, they will come to believe that it is their job to keep the family together. For the Heroic child of the alcoholic parent, life can be stressful as they will feel the need to "step up" and take responsibility for the family. In the extreme case of addiction, a teenager can feel the demand to work to help the family make ends meet or provide food for themselves and their siblings. They can also see themselves as the balancing factor of how to handle dad's drinking. Heroic children may pour beer out, flush cocaine down the toilet, or help call rideshare services when mom cannot drive.

As they get older, Heroic children will begin to find themselves in an awkward position. Not only are they the ones that family stress has rested on, but they feel a responsibility to keep things together. To make sense of their world, Heroic children can enforce their role over their parents, making them the authority on how things should be done. Why not? They seem to have things together when mom drinks every night and dad lets her. Without any other guidance, these children can be prone to a few different issues.

First, they become the guiding light in the family system. A teenager should be the final say in zero decisions for a family unit.

If both parents feel lost in their own world, then the Hero child may take their place, creating two possible scenarios. The first of these is the pseudo-parent. After years of keeping the family together, Hero children may feel the right and responsibility to shape the family and keep their parents from falling apart. Whether it is directly due to trauma or long-term family dynamics, they become the head of the emotional and relational household. In many cases, the parents let them. Their shame and discomfort have left their threats without teeth and points of view without merit. So, the Heroic child must bear the entire family's stress with a distorted worldview they have had since they were young.

In partnership with the pseudo-parent comes the pseudo-spouse. This typically happens when the same-sex parent is the addict. If a son becomes a Hero in a family system with a drug-addicted father, he may begin to play the role of spouse to his mother. She may unwittingly reinforce this idea by directing her struggles and need for connection to her son, rather than her husband or supportive people. This Heroic son then understands that he must protect his mother, even from his father if necessary. None of this is inherently sexual but is fundamentally emotional. He is the shoulder she cries on and the one to give sound advice on family needs.

The other possible downfall of the Heroic child is the burnout or shame they experience. No child is equipped for the weight of stress from their parents' relationship. After years of toil and a lack of emotional growth, the inevitable conclusion comes. They cannot be good enough to make everything right. Their drinking typically either develops in hiding or in a great rebellion. If they wish to keep their role as the Hero, they will drink in secret to avoid losing their title and image in the family. If they finally have enough and decide that no amount of stress and expectation is worth enduring any longer, they will blow out in spectacular proportion. Finally letting go of years of undue burden, they will use drugs and alcohol to their heart's content, even to the point of outright mockery of their parents.

I worry about the Heroic child in an addicted family system.

Their tendency towards keeping an image up is incredibly difficult to overcome. Without the assurance of everyone getting healthy in recovery, Heroic children struggle to show their weakness and fear. If they do hit the eject button and try to detach themselves from the family unit, they may not have the knowledge or restraint that others have. They may buy cocaine to get back at their mother and have no understanding of how much is typical in long-term addiction. Heroic children can even become so overwhelmed that the prospect of living in the world they are in or living at all becomes something they truly ponder.

The second role of a child of an addicted parent is the Villain. This child is marked by their position of terrible behavior and expectations. They begin to act out in their early years and their parents have come to expect that they will be defiant and unruly. These children must come to expect that they will be terrible children and are reinforced in this belief. This comes from parents' expectations of their failure that is expressed through either direct commentary on their terrible actions or constant questioning of motives. In more general conversation, others can end up accepting that they will continue to get in trouble and cause their parents stress. Their point of balance in the family system is that they feel the need to act out to achieve a connection to their parents. Remember, children are ignorant and only work from the information that they are given. Villainous children learn that positive behavior does not elicit the same response as negative behavior does. Since all children need connection, but Villains cannot get the loving connection, they will take the relationship they can get.

In the general world, Villains are easy to spot. They are the children constantly in trouble at school. They could even be the ones that are regularly suspended from school or even put into treatment. The halls of juvenile detention are nearly all filled with Villainous children. Almost everyone there can tell the story of how they have been in and out of trouble. Some even begin to wear this as a badge of honor in their relationships. Villains will take pride in their rebellious behavior and become so identified with antisocial behavior that they struggle to find identification with vulnerable connections. In a less extreme sense, Villainous children will be blamed for their parents' stress. To some degree, they do cause tension in their family unity. However, parents will enforce this role by blaming the child for things they did not do so that they do not have to examine their own actions or motivations.

As the Villains continue in their life and begin to grow, they end up with a problem. When they attempt to change, no one believes them. An entire family unit can be so used to them running a scheme or trying to weasel out of consequences, that if a true change were to occur, no one would accept it. From their earliest memory, Villains can come to believe that they will never change since they have no capability to do so. They become handicapped by their role and will never be able to make and keep the connections they desire since they have no training in positive social relationships and may have come to believe that they are so flawed, that no one would ever intimately connect with them and stay.

Within the addicted family system, there are unique challenges for the Villain. First, they could be blamed for the parent's substance use. These children could even hear, "See this is why you make me drink," or "Of course I use pills, I come home and am so stressed out." Villainous children can come to believe that they embody the sickness in the family system, particularly in drug or alcohol use. They bear the weight of their parent's drinking and their lack of humility to address this drinking. Like the Hero, the Villain bears the weight of the entire family and is unable to handle it. Their downfall is a full solidification of their damaged identity. At some point, they come to accept this and will engage in much of the same behavior they have seen modeled. As much as their parents may beg them to not drink or use like they do, the Villain is left with no other option.

Villains will continue this cycle of failure until it kills them. They may make attempts to right themselves, but if they do, the world becomes so unbelievably confusing that they go back to rebellion. Villainous children have no understanding of what healthy behavior or relationships are. Even those that wish to help them feel a total loss of direction. Children in this mode may be the safest addicts out of the three roles as they can understand consequences and how to work a family or legal system enough to remain sustained. Certainly not completely insulated from the risks of use, they are fluent enough in unhealthy patterns that they have some sense of peace in the world when everything is continually falling apart.

The final role of a child in an addicted family system is the Lost child. This child is known for their ability to fade into the background. Whether they go that way due to their own decision or are pushed there by the stress of the family, Lost children are ones put to the side by the family unit. What marks a Lost child most accurately is their ability to disappear from family interactions and be forgotten about. They often fade into the background to not stress other members of the family, particularly their parents. Their remarkable trait in the family system is their ability to remove themselves as a factor from an overall problem. For instance, if a sibling is becoming defiant and develops a string of rebellious behavior, a Lost child will become quieter and more compliant. Often mistaken for being independent and self-reliant, Lost children have learned that their needs will either be discredited or ignored. Instead of fighting for a connection that will not be met, they have resigned themselves to relying on their isolated abilities.

You can identify Lost children in the general population from their ability to be unnoticed. Some people can forget that a friend or a family member has a child present as they are often in their room or doing independent activities. You can also see Lost children engaging in activities that are self-reflective and require no outside input. They can develop talents or obsessions out of the knowledge or scope of their parents, making them a pariah of their family system. Lost children can also be seen in extreme circumstances if they long to be seen. After years of being forgotten, they may feel the need to be understood or not be so quiet anymore.

Lost children begin to struggle in one of two extremes or by remaining in the middle. They can become so overwhelmed by the outside world that they retreat into themselves and never allow any outside input. In an almost defiant way, Lost children can reject outside support since they have developed a pattern of isolation that has kept them from outside influence. They become so accustomed to being alone, that if someone wishes to connect with them, it can be seen as threatening to their fragile sense of safety they cling onto. On the other extreme, Lost children can become so desperate in their loneliness that they make a grand gesture to be seen or heard. After years of being forgotten, they can likely reach a point of recognition of their sadness and make a last-ditch effort to find love and support. Finally, their pattern can settle somewhere in the middle, where they accept their lot in life and move forward without seeking interconnection from hardly anyone. They may allow a few people to connect with them, but it is from a distance and with limited information.

In an addicted family system, Lost children come to understand that their most beneficial role is to not be seen or heard. If dad drinks, they go to their room and put headphones on. If mom is using drugs again, they will seem distant and uninvolved, often forgotten about or assumed to be uncaring about the family struggle. While they do care deeply, Lost children take on the burden of being forgotten so that others can get the help that they need. To be clear, this is not to pull attention away. That would be more like a Villain who focuses on how terrible they are so there is some level of connection. Lost children truly see themselves as too much for others to handle.

Of all the roles of children in an addicted family system, Lost children concern me the most. There is a buildup to a Hero falling into addiction and the Villain has a long list of treatment stints that have well-documented evidence. A Lost child has become so unremarkable to their family that if they do start to use substances themselves, no one will notice. Their addiction will fly under the radar for so long that by the time their condition has become critical, years of details and possible support has been lost. Family members of Lost addicts will often comment about how they did not know that it was happening or somehow missed the signs. It is not that the signs were not there, but that everyone was so used to ignoring the Lost child that there was no consideration for what they may be going through. If there is a Lost child within a family system, they will likely need significant support in rejoining everyone else as their downfall can easily be missed until it is much too late.

AS A PARENT OR CAREGIVER

Now we will look at the typical dynamics when the addict is the child in a family system. This section will often be related to juveniles or young adults who have recently left the home. Keeping in mind the roles of the child we just spoke about, we can then look at the ways that each child will interact as an addict. There is one thing that I would like to get out of the way. If you are a parent or someone who cares for someone that is an addict, you have likely asked yourself if you somehow caused their addiction. In short, yes. Not to the fullest degree you may be thinking, but there are certainly behaviors and patterns that could have been addressed before addiction came into their lives. I also do not want you to take away that an addict gets to blame their parents for everything wrong with them. Certainly, there is room for blame for everyone involved. There is hope in this section if you choose to read through it. You will read some very immediate and practical ways you can help them and yourselves. Near the end of this section, you will also read about long-term ways you can be a part of the positive changes needed.

First, let me unpack my earlier statement. If you are the parent or primary caregiver for a child or adolescent who is an addict, you likely hold some responsibility for their decline. I am making no assumptions about malicious intent in your parenting, nor am I implying that you have no care for your child. There is also no shame in admitting this and the acknowledgment of our own roles helps free us from the cycles of addiction and provides an opportunity for healing. You will get the building blocks for what you need to make the next steps in recovery. Our first recognition is to remember the previous experience at the Philadelphia Child Guidance Clinic. We learned that a child can be "healed" of their unruly behavior for extended periods of time if they are away from home. From a fatalistic point of view, it could be assumed that a child or adolescent should remain for years on end in treatment or even be transitioned into another place to live. This is certainly not the case. As the parents, you simply have the greatest impact on their lives; use it for their good.

There is hope for the future. Do not resign yourself to always being the problem or being a perpetual punching bag for your child. Another typical feeling from parents of addicts is the desperation to keep them alive and satisfied. Especially if your child is using substances that could be deadly, it is normal to be concerned and for the natural parental instincts of protection to come into play. There is no point in the healing process where you will stop being their parents and wanting the best for them.

So, how did we get here? How did our little girl end up throwing her life away so spectacularly over the past few years? What could we have done differently? Did we screw her up forever? Let us dispel a few concerns here. There is no single moment that caused this. No one person changed the trajectory of their life so severely that we can place the blame. Instead, there are a series of moments that come along and teach children about themselves and the world around them. So, no one moment of trauma forever ruined your child. Instead, we can consider the element of resiliency. This is the ability to deal with stress and pressure without breaking. Have you ever noticed that two children can go through the exact same ordeal, only to have completely different reactions? The key here is not what has happened, but how they were left vulnerable to not fully coping with what happened.

For whatever reason, children that become addicts have developed a chronic inability to cope with their emotions and relationships in a healthy way. This could be from lack of training, holding the anxiety of the family unit on their own, or even that their personality tended them towards estrangement in their own home. In therapy, there is an opportunity to find all the details of what led to addiction. For family systems work, I am not looking for a monster to blame. They got to this point from what they were brought into coupled with the choices they made. So, how does a child become unable to cope with the world around them? If we look at the three roles of a child in the addicted family system, we can find some clarity.

Remember, the roles of children spoken about earlier were not exclusive to addiction. In fact, those roles were theorized by researchers long before addiction came into the picture as a family systems issue. Each of those roles is enforced by family structures that are unstable with parents that are unable to support and be vulnerable with one another. Much like the obsessive pageant mom or the parents who require random drug screenings with no legitimate reason, some parents avoid their own individual or relational issues and focus on their child. Without adequate boundaries and healthy dynamics, children often bear the burden of their parents' sins. Starting with the Heroic child, they can become an addict by being overwhelmed past a tipping point. Their goal is to be good enough for the family to be stable. Once they realize that goal is unattainable, they need something extra to cope. Heroic children will often hide their addiction well and parents may not even be aware of how their child obtained such substances or alcohol. For healing the Heroic child within a family system context, the burdens and responsibilities of family support need to be lifted off their shoulders. They certainly have demands and responsibilities put upon them. That is life. Instead, they should be given responsibilities that are reasonable for a child. Do not tell a Heroic child about your relationship issues. Do not confide in them about how you are considering divorce, and certainly do not pit them against the other parent in some petty argument. I am sick of hearing adolescents and young adults in my office tell me about how they have been a messenger for their parents' unending bickering. Allow them to be three-dimensional. There is more to them than just their performance and the show they put on for others. You love them whether they succeed or fail. Remind them of that and stick through the initial shame they feel of not being able to be good enough for you.

For the Villainous child, remember that they may not be able to conceptualize healthy interaction. Their intertwining with drugs or alcohol could be so tied to their understanding of their role in the family, that they would have to shift their entire identity just to be sober. This is particularly challenging when everyone can be so used to the Villain failing, that they are suspicious of every action, even when they should not be. Villains will often comment, "Well, you think I'm using anyway, so I might as well." Statements like this show just how ingrained their belief of inability to succeed has grown. To help the Villainous addict, it is going to be important for you to regulate yourself and consider the facts of what is in front of you. They may struggle for longer to embrace recovery, but they will need someone believing in them to bridge the gap between a Villain and a normal person. It is also worth mentioning that it is okay to be suspicious. The Villain can be so used to hiding things that they conceal benevolent actions, just out of habit. They also are used to getting away with things for a while, so they may have truly relapsed when you get suspicious. The Villainous child needs you to be consistent in both boundaries and expectations. If they fail, you love them and you will be there for them, but you cannot expect failure. They can do it; it will just be a long road.

The Lost children concern me the most in addiction, particularly in family systems. If you have identified your addicted child as Lost, the first step is to take time and explore how many years of signs were missed, either through intentional distraction, or simply because you expected them to be independent and therefore were unable to witness any concerning behavior. They will likely have much to say about the family relationship but will take some time to come out with it. Lost children may have resigned themselves to isolation, so it will be important to connect with them. Swift intervention is necessary for Lost addicts. Without a proper understanding of their history and current issues, their downward spiral could easily be missed and they may be terminal much sooner than expected. Do not overwhelm them with attention and intervention, as this may signal a sign of panic and distrust. Instead, focus on a continual invitation to discussion and changing dynamics. They will be hesitant to engage, but a solid space for them to come to is integral to their recovery.

OVERALL FAMILY SYSTEM

Now that we understand the basics of family dynamics in addiction, we can make effective changes moving forward. There are a few things to get out of the way before we do. First, we need to understand where addiction comes from in the family and how it is passed. We also need to clarify how everything ends up tying together in recovery. Also, we need to set realistic expectations for everyone involved.

After years of research and decades of theory, there is no solid genetic component for addiction. Instead, there are increased risks due to family history and interactions. For those of you that need to hear that again, there is no identified gene for addiction. You did not pass this to your children through the inherent relationship with them. That can be a good thing and a bad thing. If you think back to the Medical Theory of addiction, if there is a determinable cause, then there can be targeted treatment. It is easy to fall into this trap, hoping to find someone or something to blame this tragedy on. That journey is a failing endeavor that leads to blame and the destruction of relationships.

Without genes to blame, and without specific traumas to point to, there must be a commonality. Surely there is a point when patterns play out for a reason. I mean, they are patterns. That is why they exist. Why then does addiction pop up for some people when there is no family history of it? Like much of what you have read here, remember that addiction is not special. It is something that is much like what everyone deals with, only to a more significant degree. From Attachment Theory and insight from family systems theorists, we can see a pattern of disconnection, unfortunate modeling, and a lack of coping skills predicated on past failure. While the specific drug or substance may be a result of social influence and availability, "addictive behavior" is not really a thing.

To provide some clarity to that last statement, I am tired of hearing that someone has an "addictive personality" or a pattern of "addictive behaviors." No, addiction is not like hair color or the probable length of your big toe. It is learned. Sure, there are pre-determining factors that we discussed earlier, but it is by no means an absolute result. Whenever someone reports these dynamics to me, all I can think about is how terribly lost they must feel and how fiercely they try to cling to any small ounce of hope they can find. That is not just addiction; that is true despair.

So then, how does addiction get passed down in families? For one, modeling is certainly a thing. Why do I watch basketball with my family when I do not even have cable in my own home? Why would I carry a Southern accent when I get frustrated or sleepy? These are leftovers of the way I was raised. To a similar degree, it is easy to find yourself drinking and smoking if your parents are always drinking and smoking. It is not a certainty, but it sure does make things easier. However, I would like for you to consider modeling one step past the behavioral, into the emotional. If you have ever seen a child with a filthy sailor's mouth when they do not get what they want and have been confused, only to see their parents swearing at them moments later, you can see some of this. Children can see their parents not speak about stressful or obvious issues and assume that is what is expected and healthy. While I have no concrete evidence at the time of this writing, it is fascinating to see children mimic symptoms of their parent's very real clinical issues. Kids pick up on emotional cues just as much as they pick up on behavioral ones.

Emotional modeling goes further than just from parent to child. Through our transgenerational theorists, we can see how issues can flow through families. Let me give an example. Let us assume that grandfather drank heavily, but grandmother did not. None of the children did either. Somehow, little Billy has picked up the bottle and has not been able to put it down. Instead of blaming genes, consider how the whole family has coped with issues. Grandfather drank and did not address his emotional issues. His inability to regulate and connect both destroyed his liver and wrecked any opportunity for a meaningful relationship. At some point, grandmother resigned herself to the supposed destiny of being married to a chronic alcoholic. Grandmother will have to cope in a few different ways. First, she will need to deflect responsibility because she cannot make sense of things herself, or she could put all the blame on her grandfather and avoid her own emotional deficiencies. This creates tension for the children. They learn that things will remain unresolved, and emotions should be shackled by shame until you fall apart. They can either rebel and become overly emotional or repeat the pattern. Once one of those children gets married, they keep this belief of shoving down emotions. They could maintain a romantic relationship enough to have children. Without getting help, they mimic some of the same symptoms grandmother had. Now we come to a child who was raised in a home where emotions were not flushed out, secrets were kept, and shame was an underhanded motivator. Instead of having a discussion, little Billy has no context for why he feels the way he does and has no opportunity to express it and find help. Without the parents' ability to change, they model grandmother and facilitate a mirror of grandfather in emotional connection and maturity.

If you have never heard of this kind of emotional dynamic tracking, it may be a lot to take in. Some may feel overwhelmed that they ruined their child. Others can start to make connections that they wished they were able to see before. If we want to place blame here, we can blame grandfather and grandmother, mom and dad, the school system, the judicial system, and every other person who could have done something and did not. Place this blame where you feel it needs to be. Then, once you have done that, accept where you are now and move on. If you are identifying with what you are reading, there is no going back. You are responsible for what you know and what you are offered. Here is an opportunity to see entire lifespans differently. Take that opportunity.

In a greater family system, there is also an explanation for how addiction runs in families. We will talk about triangles a bit later, which will give more clarity, but what you need to know is that when someone is unable to deal with their stuff, they push it off to something else. If you have entire family systems that are used to pushing issues onto substances, they become connected in their disconnection to emotions. When there are entire generations of families that have just accepted that drinking or using is a part of the family dynamic, it is clear what a likely result is. Using substances and avoiding vulnerability ties an entire family unit together. If one were to get sober, the entire sick homeostasis could be thrown off and the family into turmoil. So, if little Billy wants to feel connected to his family values, he will crack open a beer and tell tales much like his grandfather about his fun times when drinking. If you only get one family and the one you have smokes weed to be connected, you will probably either join them or tolerate others doing it.

Recovery throws a shiny chrome wrench into family dynamics. If the addict was a parent, then they may feel wholly unequipped to deal with the emotional stress of being sober and present. They are right. If the addict was a child, they may try to quickly veer into their previously assigned role to make sense of the world. If the addict carries the family scar, there may be no healthy way to interact with extended members of the family. Just as jarring as it can be to be thrust into sobriety, so it can be for trying to find a new way to live. Much of recovery is not talking about drugs or alcohol, but about pain and fear. It is facing the demons borne out of years of compromise, seeking out the still small light in the distance. This will take time.

When you do finally take this journey, know that relapse is a part of the process. I do not mean going back to using drugs. I mean that when you see your wife look guilty after a meeting, you will likely revert to thinking about a need for a breathalyzer. When you hear your son start to stutter when speaking about how their day went, you may immediately want to begin a full pat down and interrogative line of questioning. When your mom seems a bit sleepy during lunch, you may want to drug test her. All of this is normal thinking brought from the trauma you have experienced. If you are an addict in recovery, you will consider jumping off and finding something that has always worked for your anxiety and shame. You may start to pit your parents against one another, so they do not notice your schemes. You may feel the compulsion to lie out of habit just in case you did something wrong that you were not aware of. This is all to be expected.

The difference between someone who deals with this and someone who stays stuck depends on what they are willing to face. If you are a family member or loved one, are you able to see the possibility of success and believe that it is possible? If you are the addict, could you hope to be someone worth depending on and being close to? Is everyone involved willing to take the risk of trusting one another and seeing what is on the other side? True recovery is the violent adjustment of unhealthy roles and patterns to accommodate loving and trusting relationships. It is the ability to be exposed and know that there is worth and value in what you are and what you can expect. It is terrible, painful, and depressing at times. Yet, it is worth it. Life is better on the other side.

There is some good news here for those on the family systems train. When it comes to family roles and family dynamics, the greatest opportunity for change comes in these transitional periods, moments of change. Upon the possibility of a proverbial new day, many find their chance to try something different. If everyone agrees about a difference in a relationship, that is a transitional period. I would encourage you that even a strong conversation or setting of boundaries counts as a transitional period. When someone finally agrees to treatment, there is a window of opportunity for change. The trick is you must stick to it.

If you do wish to try something new and enact lasting change, everyone must admit that they played a role in what has come to pass. This does not include children. They are not responsible for their parents. The burden of their addiction rests upon them. Not everyone carries the same amount of blame for how things came to pass, but everyone plays a role. I do believe in free will. Each person is responsible for their own actions and should be held accountable for them. However, immediate family members, loved ones, and significant others should take time to examine their role in allowing addiction to take place. For some, this allowance comes from tolerance of unhealthy conduct. They could have said something or made a stand, but they did not. For others, their blame is most obviously shown in direct funding of substance abuse or giving money to cover expenses that should be taken care of by an addict. In extreme cases, addicts can get substances or support from family members to use.

In all of these cases, assigned roles are in place. If you are reading this book as a loved one of someone in addiction, your small act of defiance against unhealthy family dynamics is your ability to fight back. Everyone should push against the fear that they will do too little or too much. No valiant act is too small an opportunity for change, and no great declaration of expectations will derail any hope of recovery. We will talk later about specific roles for spouses and significant others, but everyone has a place in this. In some cases, you may find yourself doing everything you can to make things right. You may have gone above and beyond what could be expected. While I have no authority to, I hope to absolve you of the obligation to change someone who is not willing to do any work themselves. If this is something you are considering, find support and honest feedback, but know that you can only do what is healthy. If you have your own family and the addict is a family member or friend, know that their addiction is weighing on your relationships as well. Make a wise choice in where you put your time and energy.

For those in the recovery journey long-term, your job is the most difficult. There is not going to be full relief any time soon. There will be moments of clarity and respite, but this process is tedious and arduous. There are years of dynamics that must be addressed and layers of emotional distress that must be seen. Know that it took years to get here, but it does not take years to make a change. With effective help from therapy and recovery-minded people, much change can be made rather quickly. If the addict is 30 years old, 30 years of therapy is not needed to come to a reasonable understanding of life. Instead, know that the tough road now leads to greater results later, if you stick to what you know. Realistically, the journey of recovery is draining for everyone. Be kind to yourself and keep a connection with those that will support and guide you. There is much to change, but much hope is to be found. Accept that there will be miles ahead and yards back. If everyone is honest, vulnerable, and moving forward, I consider that a process of healing and recovery.

X&Y TRACK 4

CODEPENDENCY MAY BE one of the most overused words in pop psychology today. Everyone seems to have an opinion about who is codependent and who is not. They will even argue with great vigor that their exes were codependent and others in their life seem to be as well. The problem is that no one seems to be able to define what codependency is and what it actually means. Instead, it is used as a tool to challenge or minimize someone's emotions without consequence. Codependency is rather common both in addiction and in the general public. The funniest way I have seen this described is when someone goes on their social media page to talk about how this new person is their "whole world." The problem is two weeks ago they had a whole different one. That is not a healthy relationship; that's a solar system, and it isn't a good thing. There are many ways to spot codependency and solid ways to deal with it. So please, stop calling someone codependent because you did not like the relationship or want to feel justified in your actions. It does not work that way.

ORIGINS

So, what is codependency and how does it come about? If you read the last chapter, you can see how patterns can develop in families and affect the following generations. If you need a reminder, the basic premise is that no member of a family is isolated in their emotions or ability to influence other members. Over time, these interactions form patterns that can be tracked that show beliefs and roles in both the immediate and extended family system. After learning and internalizing these expectations of behavior, they are often translated into other relationships. For example, if a child learns that they have to be the Hero of their family system, they may try to apply that same role in friendships or romantic relationships. After some time, they could also see the desperation in this pursuit and attempt something completely opposite, expecting someone to take care of them. The Villain has understood that they are the problem in relationships and continue the paradigm or do as much as they possibly can to justify their ability to be in a relationship, attempting to become a Hero of sorts. A Lost child could carry their belief of inconsequence and try to make as little impact as possible or start to yell and scream for all the attention that they missed as a child.

Without the specific roles of children, there are general dynamics in play that can explain where codependency originated. The first comes from the general understanding of what codependency is and how it comes about. In the most basic sense, it is the need for someone else to be present to feel stable and understand what is happening in the world. This is not simply the need for someone to explain what is happening in a frightening situation. Instead, this is the inability to cope with emotions independently. It is a lack of self-identity that leads to a deep feeling of being incomplete and unable to move forward. In family dynamics, children are much like this. They have no idea what the world holds and need someone to hold their hand and make sense of what is happening. Children have little identity on their own and need to be guided on what behaviors are helpful for them and which ones will ultimately make their lives more difficult. The hope is that these children will grow out of this utter dependence on their parents and find their own way.

When they do not gain the ability to make sense of the world on their own, they are left to follow the directions of their social circles, from friends to significant others. Today, this has extended into social media as well. This is different from the normal progression that everyone goes through. All of us had times when we were more influenced by our peers than we would be proud to admit. We also attempted to find our own voice in this realm to shape who we are. Budding codependent behavior is different. Instead of looking to friends and significant others for signals on how to proceed in life, codependent people take orders on what they should do and think. It may not be a direct command of specific actions, but they infer what is needed from others' cues so that they can belong to a group and continue the connections that they are holding so tightly onto.

For some, this is where the introduction to addiction comes to light. More than just simple acceptance, involvement in drugs and alcohol can easily be required for social groups that foster codependent relationships. Many have shared a similar story of how friends or significant others encouraged their use. At some point, it became less about fitting in and more about needing it to be present. Others feel such great strain from an insecure relationship with their peers that they seek ways to cope that are acceptable. There are even common sayings about people like this. "Jimmy may drink too much sometimes, but that's just him." "Sally sure can put down a lot, but she has always been that way and she probably won't change." An addiction that grows out of this stage may be some of the most difficult to spot since addicts are often embedded in social circles that enable and support their destructive behavior. It is difficult to see that there is a problem if everyone says you are fine, and they engage in addictive patterns sometimes themselves.

Another projection of codependency can come from when children continue codependent behavior with their parents. The pseudo-spouse and pseudo-parent both exemplify the codependent dynamic with little hope for change other than an emotional disconnection from affected family members altogether. The pseudo-spouse engages in a role they are not suited or equipped for. These children must shoulder the burden of their parent's failed relationships and provide a listening ear whenever one of the parents falls apart. The child who assumes the role of a pseudo-spouse is crippled by their inability to disconnect from their parent, leaving them without experience or confidence in other relationships. The blame for this rests on both parents. The pseudo-parent endures a similar duty of caring for their parent but to a greater degree. A child not only has to assume the role of a supporter but also a caregiver to a capable yet inconsolable parent. They may feel a greater degree of a lost childhood so that they could "grow up" enough to support their family unit either emotionally or physically. The pseudo-parent has a sharper role that is more direct and easily defined, but the pseudo-spouse may have more difficulty finding the ability to change with the hazy boundaries and expectations that are largely unspoken. In short, these children were trained to be unhealthy and incapable of independence.

There are a couple of other examples worth mentioning in the family system's breeding of codependency. For one, codependency can be borne out of genuine need. If there is a loss of one parent and finances are tough, children may have to pull weight in work or support in other ways. Another possibility is when one child is abnormally sick, and their siblings are not. The one who is sick may need constant attention and care just to be able to function. The short-term change in family dynamics of hyperfocus on one child and missed opportunities with others can create codependent dynamics, but these do not result from laziness or an inability to take responsibility. To the parent reading this who wonders if their family dynamic could have contributed to codependent patterns in their children, listen carefully. If you can honestly say that the things that you did were the best you could do to simply keep your head above water, if you can truly look back on your motivations and see that you lost yourself in a pursuit to help others, never wanting to burden them and now are seeing codependent behavior, take a breath. This form of codependency is more easily worked on in therapy as time goes on. Children learn about the world and their upbringing as they get older and move out. They can come to understand that the dynamics that they experienced were not ideal and were detrimental at times. Children can come to appreciate the complexity of life as they mature. Codependency is mostly learned, but with honest effort, it is effectively dealt with.

TRIANGULATION

Upbringing seems to have a significant effect on codependency through roles that are encouraged and enforced. How do children learn this? It is rarely the case that a parent comes out and demands that certain changes be made to a dynamic and that a child is required to fill a role that they are not equipped for. Furthermore, how could an addicted child learn unhealthy relationship patterns with parents that have never had any issues with substances or alcohol? The answer comes from my favorite geometrical shape in all of therapy—the triangle.

I will admit two things. When I talk about shapes in therapy and ask what a client thinks my favorite is, I sometimes get the answer of a square because people like to crack jokes and try to make fun of me. Haha, I'm boring and in my free time, I like to sit in my office, play guitar with headphones on, and not talk to anyone. Funny. They all seem to think they are original for that one. The other thing to admit is that the idea of triangles comes from a wonderful theorist and researcher named Murray Bowen. He originally intended this idea to encompass family systems issues, but I borrowed it from him to help addicts understand the function of their addiction. The idea of triangulation is incredibly interesting and encouraging. If this concept makes sense to you, there is a good chance that you will begin to see it everywhere you go and in relationships that you observe.

Triangulation is a rather simple idea. Ideally, two people, called a dyad, would have continual feedback and a free-flowing relationship. They could give information to each other, challenge each other, and build a relationship that grows over time. The negative version is a disconnection in open communication that results in secrets and power plays. If they are unable to maintain the healthy version of a relationship and move to the unhealthy version, they need something to stabilize them. Dyads can either leave each other or find something to balance their stress. The easiest way to conceptualize this is through a bicycle.

Two tires represent a dyad, and a frame is what connects them together. If the bike is moving, it remains upright. The movement represents the growing relationship and active work it takes to kindle a healthy connection and keep the bicycle upright. A vulnerable relationship requires continued work in which each member constantly moves forward. If something happens and movement no longer occurs, it is a good idea to try to keep the bike in the upright position. To solve this problem, a kickstand can be used. The tires no longer need to move, and the dyad no longer needs to work on their relationship issues. Instead, this kickstand will keep the whole relationship stable. Dyadic relationships with open and vulnerable connections are healthy, but not stable without continued work. Triangulated relationships are incredibly stable, but not healthy.

A bicycle is getting no use out of just remaining upright without any form of movement or engagement. It is still present and able to be used but remains stationary with the support of a kickstand. The triangle is formed when the dyad relies on a third party to stabilize the relationship. This third party can be many different things. I will give some examples, but really anything can fill this void. Two examples were given in the previous chapter about unhealthy family dynamics that parents can have with their children—travel baseball and child pageantry. Again, not every set of parents involved in these activities is terrible, codependent, and triangulating their children. They can be some very obvious examples of triangulation and using children as a kickstand. In both cases, parents are using their children to avoid their individual and relational issues.

Starting with travel baseball, there is always that one dad who is so engrossed in the success of his son that it seems to be an exercise in vicarious living. Whether dad is reliving his glory days that he never grew out of or is wanting his son to achieve what he never could, this guy is one of the greatest reasons that umpires need blood pressure medication. Much more than just passion for the sport, this dad seems to stake his entire being on the outcome of a little league game. When he has boxed his son so thoroughly into the ballplayer ideal that there is no other way to interact with him, game nights in high school become a nightmare for every other parent in the stands. Dad could coach way better and the school's coaches are benching his son because they are stupid and want to lose, apparently. Mom on the other hand either joins in or retreats in embarrassment for what her husband has become. The two are unable to resolve their issues and deal with emotional problems. At some point, things can become so volatile that hardly a word is spoken between the two of them. The only point of conversation is their son's budding baseball career. Over time, they have lost all semblance of a relationship between the two of them. The only thing that is left is the rusty kickstand they call a son.

Pageantry can be much the same, but with different details. Maybe this is more of just a Southern American thing, but something about parading around a four-year-old as the most amazing human being to grace a stage is off-putting. Some couples can make their entire relationship and schedule so engrossed in pageant trips that they will spend thousands on a dress with a five-hundred-dollar prize pool that the child will grow out of in two months. Meanwhile, bills can be piling up past the point of reasonability. The point of similarity in both of these cases is the neglect of a real relationship that encourages, supports, and challenges one another. This can spill over into legitimate financial and social burdens, with the sole focus on a wounded child. Without this child fulfilling their role, there would be no relationship left.

In more typical cases of triangulation in parents, there is a breaking point that always shows, when all the children leave the home. Beyond the early years of marriage, this is one of the times of increased divorce rates. Some parents have spent most of their adulthood leaving themselves and their spouse in a realm of neglect, that when the children leave and the kickstand is taken away, the bike can no longer function. Gears have long been rusted and the chain is broken. Any attempt to make that bicycle move again will go nowhere. Some do not realize this until it is too late, until everyone is moved out and they sit down with their spouse of over two decades. When it is just the two of them, they have no idea who they are or who the other person is. Many describe this as growing apart, and in some ways it is. Leaving a bike out in the rain for years and only focusing on polishing a kickstand is disastrous and depressing. The once beautiful and strong symbol of movement has become decrepit and unrecognizable. Many couples will only be able to see their children as a source of hope and their long-time partner is some new person whom they have not paid attention to for so long, and people can change a lot in twenty years.

Triangulation at its core is little more than anxiety dispersal. It is the desire to place our own need to have community and support and outsourcing pressure to someone or something else. Anything can fill this spot from someone's job, to a belief system, to traumatic experiences. A person can become so engrossed in their job that they are unable to truly connect with others and use their employment as a way to avoid confrontation. We call those people workaholics. Others can use their beliefs as a shield from any true connection to a partner or forms of criticism. We call those people fanatics. Still, others can connect through high-stress situations or moments of trauma. We call those people coworkers in the service industry. Whatever that triangulated thing is, when it is gone, dyads no longer know how to interact.

When looking at addiction specifically, triangulation is most aptly described by a term I call the mitigating factor. Interchangeable by nearly everything that exists, the mitigating factor is that kickstand talked about earlier. It is the thing that keeps each member of a dyad from truly interacting with one another in true vulnerability and engagement. Instead of one partner communicating with the other, they feel as if a gap is present, and energy is gone from the relationship. Instead of finding a resolution between each other, the normal relationship connection is sent out to something or someone else. I will talk about this more in the next chapter, but a third person, a mistress for example, can be a mitigating factor. To be a true mitigating factor, it has to suck the energy out of the relationship. It will create distress to the point where one partner will run to the mitigating factor to release stress and the other will see that they are missing and run to the mitigating factor as well. This third party sucks emotional vulnerability out of a relationship. Instead, it ends up increasing emotional intensity.

From here on out through this chapter, consider the mitigating factor a point of intensity. At the beginning of the chapter, there was a comment about someone building their own solar system of significant others. They are a perfect representation of emotional intensity. Those that are unable to connect in true vulnerability end up needing grand gestures to feel connected. The flighty twenty-something always in a whirlwind romance finds true vulnerability and stability impossible, so they take intensity for as long as they can. Once that runs out, the relationship is dead. They can never settle down in a perpetual triangulation; their need for intense emotional connection will not let them.

Enough with the depressing observation of inconsistent modern relationships. Let's move to something more peaceful, like an addiction. Triangulation can be incredibly easy to see if the drug or alcohol is known to be present. Let's use an alcoholic named Gary and his wife Linda. Now, Gary is a raging alcoholic who has been supported by his wife Linda. She does not like his drinking or what he becomes when he does drink. Instead, she helps deal with the fallout from a decades-long failed relationship. Since the two of them cannot retain any true connection, they have traded intimacy for intensity. This is a trade all addicts make. They have no ability to be safely connected to a significant other but still need connection. Intensity can do the job and make Gary feel wanted and cared for rather quickly. Linda feels the closest to Gary after huge consequences and Gary seems to be open and caring when he feels ashamed of the drinking from the night before. The problem is that when Gary and Linda cannot connect individually, Gary goes to his mitigating factor, his mistress, Brandy.

By the way, that is one of my favorite alcoholic jokes in therapy. So, take the time to sit and laugh about that one.

Linda feels that her husband is inaccessible through normal means and must either fight Brandy for her intoxicating effects on him or use that relationship as a way to connect. If Gary is not going to stop drinking and Linda feels powerless and alone, she can count on attempting to control the amount of hidden liquor in the house to make her feel better. Without realizing it, Linda has also traded intimacy for intensity. Her life has become so wrapped in alcoholism that she either feels on edge or completely numb. She can only fight for small moments of connection with a man that left many years ago.

There can also be triangulation between generations. In this next example, I will call the mother Cindy and the daughter Betty. Using Xanax as a mitigating factor, Betty can feel helpless to help her mother, Cindy. Cindy feels so ashamed of what she has become as a mother, that little pills are the only thing that can make her forget. Betty has reached for her mother's care for years, hoping to find a hug back from someone who swears she loves her. In an act of defiance, Betty can search through Cindy's drawers and hope to find a stash of pills to flush. Cindy can even use her biological withdrawal symptoms and need for cash to connect with her daughter and guilt her into speaking on the phone. In the end, no true relationship remains. No vulnerability is experienced, only a synthetic connection pumped by intensity. Once intensity is the only thing that is keeping them together, all that is left are memories and some distant hope for the future that may never come.

GIVERS AND TAKERS

This final depiction of codependency is probably new to many people. It comes out of my own practice and theory, as well as an understanding of systems theory and relational needs. Building from learned traits in codependency and triangulation, two different roles play out in a codependent relationship, and they are both present in any long-term dynamic. Neither one of them is better than the other. It may seem that way at first, but make sure you read through this section before you come to any conclusions. I do not have the time, money, or patience to research exactly how it happens, but there is some subconscious way that both sides of this relationship find each other. It's like a sickening magnetism. The two roles in codependency are Givers and Takers. Somehow, they always find each other and are attracted to one another.

Givers exist in codependent relationships to help, support, and offer themselves as energy for someone. They may seem selfless at first, but Givers struggle with the ability to form boundaries. They have learned connection through, well, giving themselves to others. Givers are not simply trying to be nice and helpful. Instead, they are unsure how to navigate a relationship without supporting and sacrificing. They can feel lost in their identity and stability if they cannot hand themselves over and fall on a sword to support someone else. While Givers can often be praised for their "long-suffering" efforts in a relationship, if they were honest, they need their counterpart to have standing in the world. There is no making sense of trauma or finding a way forward without an accompanied Taker.

You can see Givers being grown young when parents either deliberately or covertly require that their children support them. This is more than just a financial responsibility. A parent who does not get the support they need from family, friends, or their significant other can pull emotional support from their child. The budding Giver sees that their worth comes from their ability to produce for someone else and help them deal with their stress. Givers are also seen in teenagers when they say that they can fix someone or give them the support that they need to be great. The classic line, with no intended gendered overtones here, is "I can fix him." Over time, what was continued support becomes wholesale devotion to what someone else wants and needs. Their connection to their respective Taker hinges on their ability to be good enough to make them happy.

On the surface, Givers can appear as virtuous partners that only want the best for their significant other. However, there are many underlying concerns here. First, a Giver can focus on their partner to distract from their own issues. Without attention focused on them, they can both avoid things that are too difficult, or obscure deeper things they are trying to hide. Givers can even blame the Takers for issues when they hold responsibility for refusing to address their own issues by hyper-focusing on something else. They can also become so avoidant of their loneliness that when they are left alone, they become unable to address emotions due to a lack of recent experience. To be fair, there are positive elements in the place of a Giver. They may truly have a heart for other people and find meaning in growth. It is when this goes too far that codependency starts to become relevant.

The counterpart to the Giver is the Taker. Again, this role may seem negative compared to the Giver. There are surely negative connotations to removing energy from someone else. Takers seem unable to achieve all of the things that they need to without support from another person. This is not just normal encouragement and guidance, but something deeper. Takers feel a sense of emptiness alone and attempt to fill their needs by receiving unconditional emotional energy from someone else. Like a gas tank running on empty, Takers are constantly in need of the energy of a Giver to stay afloat. Their continual running on fumes causes great stress for themselves, but also makes them desperate to attach to a partner to make sense of the world. Without an unyielding partner, they suffer from an inability to achieve normal goals.

Takers can be developed in a couple of different ways. The first is through generalized training. Young Takers can find that everyone around them thinks they are amazing and will be something incredible. They are often doted on with continual encouragement. Their relationship with their parents often hinges on their flooding of support and the inflation of their ego. Over time, they begin to believe that they either deserve this continual praise, becoming entitled and detached from vulnerability from others, or they need such great praise because they are inherently broken.

This second guidance into being a Taker comes from a child's belief that they are incapable of doing things on their own, leading them to need constant praise and support. As they grow, they can be spotted by hearing phrases like "ride or die" and "loving big." Their connection to a Giver hinges on how much they feel supported to achieve great things or not feel so empty in their lack of ability.

From this description alone, the Taker can seem like the narcissistic jerk ex that took everything from their partner. It is easy to point fingers at the Taker, but they had a willing partner here. Underlying concerns of the Taker tend to be related to a veneer of greatness that has to be maintained, or the avoidance of just how terrible they may actually be. Takers will generally feel like they are always at the edge of a ledge, about to jump. Their identity can come from needing rescue and support, as well as inflation of their façade of a self-image. Takers are not one-sided. They can provide wonderful windows into the progress of a relationship and will give tokens of support to their Giver either through actions or tangible things. Almost if they need to prove that the work has paid off, Takers will need to show that they are worthy of being supported and will guard the perception of their success very carefully. Takers do have positive elements. Great progress in real-life changes can give support to their continued need. Takers can even support others as a way of validating their continued efforts. Their sense of achievement can be shared with the Giver, producing confidence from each partner that the suffering is worth the progress that is made.

Now that we understand the partnered roles, it is important to know that being a Giver or a Taker is not a static identity. These roles can differ between multiple relationships and also swap in character between romantic relationships over time. When working on codependency, it is important to track where changes happen and how roles can shift between concurrent relationships. Going back to the family dynamic, multiple roles can be held at the same time for parents and children. Using Gary and Linda's story again, triangulation and codependency are easily seen. Alcohol exists as the mitigating factor that balances the relationship. Gary is the Taker, not allowing Linda to reach him emotionally. He is barely keeping himself stable. Linda is the Giver, hoping to be good enough to get Gary to stop drinking and come back to the marriage. The roles here are set and the relationship is unlikely to change without significant intervention. Due to her lack of support and inability to find stability, Linda can then become a Taker when relating to her children, using them as a source of energy to keep going. So, when speaking with her husband, Linda is a full-on Giver, losing more of herself every day with some small hope that change will come. With her children, Linda is a pitied Taker, constantly needing reassurance from the only other sober humans in the home.

An individual's codependent role can also shift in transition to new relationships. If Gary and Linda were to divorce, Linda could end up flipping her role. She could move from the wife that was drained of every ounce of her being, into someone that is so empty that she has to draw as much as possible from every romantic relationship she pursues in the future, becoming a mirror of the husband she loathed. Gary may end up feeling so dejected from his utter failure as a husband, that he fully embraces his self-hatred and refuses to request any measure of help or support from anyone else. Gary may become so ashamed of what he has done, that even in dating, and speaking to his children, he does not allow anyone in, lest he burdens the conscience of another, becoming the ultimate Giver, like his wife.

While these scenarios are incredibly sterile and extreme, varying degrees of giving and taking exist throughout all codependent relationships. One of the true measures of the severity of addiction and its resilience to treatment comes not from biology, but from adherence to this codependent triangle. With anything able to fill the mitigating factor, cross-addiction and transition into other unhealthy coping mechanisms are common. The remorseful addict can be so attached to a recovery program that they refuse vulnerable connections elsewhere. Some move their drug from cocaine to meetings, making them their only source of comfort and reprieve, isolating everyone that loves them and continuing the role of a Taker without anyone being able to argue for change. At least they are sober.

When it comes to addiction and codependency, some factors are set in stone, and others carry a high likelihood. First, all addicts are codependent, period. Look back at what has been said about codependency and triangulation. The fact that alcohol, drugs, or something else fill the role of emotional support, by definition, makes for a codependent relationship. All of their partners are codependent as well, period. The very word codependent means that two people are involved. You cannot be codependent alone. It does not work that way. If you are reading this as the loved one or significant other of someone in active addiction, you are going to need to accept that continuing the relationship with them as it has been will result in stabilization in their addiction and deterioration of your sanity. You do no good by playing a corresponding role. All addicts are codependent, and all of their significant others are as well. Their family members and loved ones will also show codependent characteristics. If the addict has children, they have been significantly trained in the mechanisms of codependency and will need long-term support to enable healthy relationships.

Moving to specific roles in codependency, most addicts will identify as strict Takers. At a minimum, they tend more towards being a Taker in the majority of their relationships. If they are in a relationship with someone who is also in their own form of addiction, they could fulfill the role of Giver as well, but this would be a limited degree of giving. It is easy to see the taking in an addict. They suck the life out of everyone around them, giving nothing of substance in return. Understanding this does not fix the issue. Codependency requires two people. We as human beings were made for connection and community. No one can truly be alone and fulfilled. Codependency is the perversion of natural connection into a forced narrative. When an addict plays the role of a Taker, they are forcing an interaction that is nearly impossible to step out of. Someone in active addiction may make threats or statements of remorse in a grand gesture to gain the connection they need to feel alive. In the most extreme sense, a Taker can threaten suicide or overdose as a means of connection to the enforced Givers they are connected to. How does a loving mother look at her son who is threatening to kill himself over withdrawal symptoms and turn away? What can a husband do when his wife is talking about taking a whole bottle of painkillers to deal with the stress of the marriage?

Addiction exists as one of the most extreme versions of codependency. Addicts have cornered themselves, pigeonholed their identity into being lost of soul, completely alone. Their recognition of failure, coupled with the human need to connect, leaves only desperate attempts to find love and connection. When they cannot find unconditional support for their transgressions from a loving partner, they will turn to the bottle. Maybe the bottle will love them or fake it long enough to forget. Maybe if they just keep pushing, someone may reach down into the pit they are in and pull them out. No one seems willing to help. So, with the alienation of true connection and inability to look inward due to overwhelming shame, there only exists moments of intoxication and the terrifying space in-between that screams shrieking reminders of their complete failure as a spouse, parent, child, friend, or human being. They cannot fathom what a real hug could feel like, only what can keep their mind off the ever-encroaching sorrow on the horizon.

I feel it appropriate to point out that this is the point of sobriety that most people do not recognize. Sure, the biological factors in sobriety will cause all kinds of symptoms that need continual observation. Still, those who have experienced true addiction will know that there is sobriety of the body and sobriety in emotions. What they are describing is the removal of the kickstand, the absence of a mitigating factor. When the world gets loud and bright again, it is not that relationships have changed, but that there is no third party to send emotional stress to. So, once an addict has detoxed from substances through medical taper, the only tendency towards use is this emotional instability. She will not relapse because of craving the biological components of heroin again; she will relapse because the black hole of despair has crept up and a mitigating factor seems like the only way to make the world quiet again.

Why do addicts use drugs and alcohol when they know it could kill them? It is safer to inject an infected needle than it is to truly look upon the lost child screaming for someone to help them, only to have the void looking back. Total rejection and anguish are more terrifying than death.

AND THREE-QUARTERS, IT MATTERS

O F ALL THE warnings I could give about the soapboxes of mine, this chapter holds the sudsiest of them. Many aspects of addiction theory and literature are well flushed out and are supported by years of study and personal experience. Particularly around individual experiences and the treatment useful for long-term sobriety, addiction literature abounds. It also seems to be the case that everyone and their brother has a book or commentary on how to have a healthy relationship, or even a podcast they boast about. Still, much has come through in understanding couple relationships and systemic dynamics. Many have been guided through dire situations with effective therapy and support. What hurts as a therapist who focuses on addiction and coupled relationships is to see that there is nearly no overlap between these two camps. The couples therapists do not want to work with addicts. They lie, cheat, and manipulate. Addiction therapists do not want to work with couples as they become complicated and can impede recovery goals. Due to the lack of information about support for the partner of the addict, you will read support for them in this chapter to help offset the loss they may feel about how to explain their situation or what to do next. I also hope to speak to the gap, those that have missed the other side, and find hope for couples that may only be holding on by a thread.

INFIDELITY

To be forthcoming and honest, I will be rather abrupt about my beliefs and theories with couples. Explanations will come along the way, but know that seemingly outlandish statements may come across the page. The first of these stark beliefs is that if someone is an addict and claims to be in a committed relationship, they have emotionally cheated on their partner. There is no exception and no outlier. If you have found yourself reactive to that statement, go back to the previous chapter and follow through with the logic of triangulation and mitigating factors. By logical processes in this book, there is no other way to see true addiction. If you are reading this as the addict, your partner will begrudgingly agree with what is written next.

In my years of working with addicts and their significant others, I have never had any partner truly disagree with me about addiction feeling like an emotional affair. When the girlfriend wonders where her partner went emotionally, she may start to wonder if cheating is present, if there is someone else in the picture. She may even drive herself crazy trying to figure out what is going on. Whatever conclusions she came to or lies she was told, there is one thing for sure; the emotional exchange in the relationship is imbalanced. It is almost as if the addicted partner swings between emotional absence and hyperfocus. She will feel a constant imbalance in her emotional state and imbalance in the ground she walks. Clearly, something else is going on. The husband may wonder if his wife is stepping out on him, avoiding answers about her behavior, and becoming more secretive. Mitigating factors leech emotions and vulnerability away from relationships, leaving only a husk of a wife to connect with her husband. This emotional absence is what relates to the feeling of an emotional affair. She is running to a bottle, to Jack, to deal with her emotions. Many affected partners wish that the mitigating factor was another person. That way, they could be mad at someone and do something about it. Instead, they are left wondering how chemicals seem to be a more fulfilling partner than they are.

Here is where we will borrow some from the systemic theorists. Infidelity work is difficult and requires significant structure. There are clearly defined rules and processes to continue in therapy, as well as expectations for each member of a couple. We will not outline all of the different steps and techniques but will review the important parts to keep in mind. I am going to use some shorthand to make things easier to understand. For the person either in the middle of or recently out of active addiction, they will be called the addicted partner. Their sober spouse or significant other will be called the grieved partner. The drug or alcohol will be called the mitigating factor or third-party depending on context. Remember, mitigating factors and third parties can change to other things or people. They only exist to spread out anxiety and avoid vulnerability.

From the addiction camp, we will borrow language around sobriety, recovery, and relapse. Sobriety is abstinence from any drugs or alcohol. Recovery is the continual process to remain sober and build a better life. Relapse is the re-engagement of drug or alcohol use. There are many theories on what constitutes relapse, but that is another topic for another book. There will also be pushback to some of the common beliefs surrounding what healthy recovery is and how it can be obtained. I fully understand that I have angered half my audience with previous chapters, and the rest will probably send me angry emails about this one. I do not care. It is my book, and I will write about what I have seen. I can only attest to that.

Assuming that you are on board with all of this, there is one more thing to mention. Infidelity is used in an emotional context here. It can also extend into physical and relational infidelity, as addiction sometimes can. For those cases, there will be some further explanation. These cases still fit the mold that we discussed previously. If the addicted partner is used to drinking to deal with issues and a breathalyzer is installed in her car, drinking is more difficult. Although, she could always start confiding in her human ex, Jack, about her problems in her marriage. Both serve a similar purpose, avoiding vulnerability and accountability, so we will treat them as the same for this chapter.

Marrying these two camps, we come to some initial conclusions. The grieved partner has felt left out of the relationship, pushed to confusion, and without much explanation. They will feel as if they were lied to, manipulated, and devalued. They have been. Grieved partners describe feelings of second-class citizenship. After years of a committed relationship, they are put to the side and replaced by the drug or alcohol. They should be affirmed in this feeling. Addiction is confusing for everyone involved, and without anyone to place the blame on, it can feel as if there is no real argument to be had. An affair partner can be blamed, yelled at, and interacted with. How can you yell at liquor? Does cocaine hear you when you are finally fed up? Sure, they are cheating, but to fight against a chemical affair partner is like grasping at vapor. It is there, but it cannot be tangibly held and leaves you wondering what exactly you are mad at in the first place. A baseline for engagement with the grieved partner is an acknowledgment of their frustration and validation of their fears of being isolated and thrown to the side.

The addicted partner needs an explanation of what healthy jealousy is and how they cheated on their partner, even if they never spoke to another person. This can seem odd at first, but once they see that the grieved partner identifies with this, they tend to come around. It is hard enough to admit to infidelity, but not knowing that you were cheating is another hurdle to deal with. The addicted partner can also feel completely shaken without their affair partner to mitigate their stressors, leaving them volatile in their relationship with the grieved partner. Everything that they could not deal with emotionally, now is more intense and without the same escape. Some level of empathy is encouraged here as recovery in itself is a daunting task, but a vulnerable relationship with the person they cheated on is even more difficult. They should be ushered compassionately into this new relationship dynamic. They are responsible for their actions but need time to adjust to a new level of emotional intensity.

Here is where a conflict arises. I will side with the relational theorists here. Many in early recovery will be told that their recovery should come first. Grieved partners are told in the process of infidelity work that they are given allowances to gain stability and control in the relationship, within reason of course. Addicts in early recovery are often told that they should consider recovery their top priority. If they do not, then they will lose everything else. Some of this is admirable. If the wife relapses, she is likely to lose her marriage and children. This order of priority is often given due to the difficulty and disconnection with significant others. Unfortunately, this tends to alienate the grieved partner.

To accommodate this, the grieved partner should have significant say in expectations of recovery. They do not need to know every detail of meetings, groups, or therapy appointments. However, they have spent possible years in the dark about what is going on. Asking them to just trust the process with no information or feedback is cruel. In isolated infidelity work, allowances are given with social media, cell phones, and other forms of communication. The goal is not to create a "helicopter parent" type of relationship, but one where the grieved partner can feel as if the ground is stable beneath them. This should taper off with time. In translation to addiction treatment with couples, the grieved partner should be allowed to consider options such as a breathalyzer installed in a car, regular drug tests, and even confirmation of medication appointments that prevent further drug or alcohol use. To the addict reading this, you may feel frustrated or angry. Sorry. You cheated on them for years. That one's on you. They get six months of consideration. Your humility and acceptance here will pay off in the long run. Take it in stride, and know that this should not be the dynamic as time goes on.

In a more direct form of critique, I understand the reasons that recovery programs have for not including partners in recovery meetings and dynamics. I get it. Partners can be volatile and disruptive. Shame is used to manipulate the addict and can drive them further into isolation and possible relapse. Partners may also lack empathy for the difficulty of addiction and the process of recovery. However, the continuation of distance from the grieved partner is counterproductive to long-term recovery and isolates the individual most harmed by the addict. If grieved partners carry so much weight in recovery, then it would make sense to include them in the process, not a side project that informs them about what is happening and what they should do. Each partner can go to a recovery meeting, get good information, go home with no discussion, and be driven further apart. This is related to what we know about systems work and couples therapy. If each member of a couple gets individual therapy, but no couples therapy, they are more likely to divorce than if they were to get no therapy at all. The dynamic that insulates the addict to keep them from relapsing also isolates the grieved partner.

Probably the most significant problem with disconnected support is the continuation of a mitigating factor. The husband just moved from alcohol to meetings to deal with his issues. Granted, a meeting probably won't kill him, but it certainly does not bring him closer to his wife. Full engagement in recovery services without returning with a new relationship often creates an unchallenged mitigating factor, leading to a continued disconnection much like addiction was. The thing is, the addicted partner is now sober. What can the grieved partner argue about in this? They got what they wanted. Their partner is sober and working on themselves. Even still, the addicted partner is drifting further away into a world that does not include them. Before, addiction was stealing them away. Now recovery is drifting them away. Truly helpful recovery services should include support and investment from a committed long-term partner. Simply put, if recovery services were to require that addicts return to their relationship and engage in what was discussed, then many more issues could be resolved. Instead, grieved partners can often feel as if their spouse is truly gone and there is no way to get them back. At least they are alive, even if they are still cheating in some way.

BOUNDARIES

So, how do couples find common ground and what can a grieved partner do to maintain balance in the relationship? In the middle of active addiction, many lines are drawn in the sand. Some of these are real, and some are empty threats. This jockeying of position is common when addiction throws a relationship into chaos, when little influence can be seen by the grieved partner. Before examining what can be done in a couple's dynamic, we need to make sure we are on the same page when speaking about interventions. The main two options that are available to the grieved partner are ultimatums and boundaries. Both attempt to change the relationship and push towards something more connected, but they go about it in very different ways, even if they sound similar on the surface.

Ultimatums are the most common form of intervention from grieved partners. There are a few surefire ways to identify an ultimatum. The first is the emotional intensity with which an ultimatum is given. These attempts to connect are often in the middle of a grand argument or when some great consequence has come about. Ultimatums are given in the heat of the moment when grieved partners feel assured in their legitimacy. Some examples of this are statements like, "That's it, I'm leaving!" or "If I catch you one more time, that's it!" Often general and without specific follow-up, ultimatums are thought of in the moment, without outside consideration or support. They can seem effective enough at first but fail in a few different ways.

The first failure is that ultimatums are threats, not options with ramifications. Long-term consequences are not thought about and in-the-moment feelings are considered the greatest truth. Without sustainability, ultimatums end up looking weak, with none of the follow-ups that were espoused when the argument was still raging. Ultimatums have no real strength and no lasting effect. They fizzle out in their usefulness as time moves on and each member of the couple cools down. This lack of strength makes ultimatums seem intense, but temporary, only frustrating the grieved partner more. With this desperation comes the second issue with ultimatums, a lack of faith that anything can change. If grieved partners were honest, they do not have faith or strength for extended interactions or vulnerable work. All they can hope for is a jolt of energy that can shock the addicted partner into changing. Some grieved partners hide behind ultimatums to avoid their own issues within the relationship. That way a grieved partner can claim that they have asked the addicted partner to change, even without any real effort. The final flaw in ultimatums is that the grieved partners that give them know they will not follow through on them. Ultimatums are a doomed endeavor, and grieved partners know that. They may feel it is all the strength they can muster to scream into the void for a small chance at change.

Boundaries are distinctly different from ultimatums, even though implementation can seem similar. Boundaries are created in times of calm when the addicted partner is not influencing the situation and no crisis is occurring. That way, the grieved partner can truly consider what they want and what they are willing to push for in the relationship. They can also think about how much more they can take. Once boundaries are thought about, they should be discussed with an emotionally stable person who understands different aspects of addiction. Boundaries honor someone's wants and needs, not their impulses. They should be clear and easily explained. The most important part of boundaries is that they are implemented, no matter the future circumstances. Boundaries should be well understood by outside supportive people in the situation that are ready to follow through on the possible recourse if necessary. Without judgment, without severe anxiety, a true boundary is recognized when the addicted partner breaks the promises made and the grieved partner follows through on consequences without guilt or shame.

With a better understanding of the difference between ultimatums and boundaries, we can look at what a real boundary is. The best way I have been able to describe healthy boundaries is from a fence. There are three parts of a fence that are important to build an effective boundary. The first is the posts that are in the ground.

Stabilizing the rest of the structure and giving a significant foundation, posts are the key markers of where the fence is built and what dimensions are required. In a boundary, posts are core beliefs and identities. They are what keeps someone grounded in their lives and their understanding of the world. Some posts may be general, like the expectation of being treated fairly, a specific religious belief, or the demand for emotional engagement. Others may be specific, such as the expectation of no screaming or violence, the expectation of a balanced marriage, or the engagement of what is necessary for the household or children. It is important to remember that posts are placed in the ground. You do not beat someone with a fencepost. Then it is no longer a fence post; it is assault. So, beliefs should not be used as a weapon, but as a statement of value that is not up for debate at this time. Grieved partners may feel as if their posts have been pushed down and become rotten. If this is you, I would encourage reaching out to someone who can relate to finding appropriate posts and where to find them if they seem lost.

The next part of a fence that is important for boundaries is the horizontal boards. These boards represent the details of life that bind together important beliefs. They are the aspects important to healthy boundaries. These boards can be replaced over time as circumstances and people change, but they should not be torn down without permission. That's vandalism. They surround the person, making fence posts valuable. Without these boards, there are just beliefs with no protection, and no way to differentiate between what is okay and what is not. Some examples of these include expectations of inclusion in recovery meetings, required drug testing, required couple's therapy, or even not allowing substances within the walls of a house. Remember, posts are only useful when they are applied. Boards work much the same way. I would not consider a board leaned up against a fence post to be of much use. They must be nailed in with sturdy resistance to pressure. There should be great effort and consideration to remove these boards if requirements in the relationship should change.

The final piece of this fence analogy is the clearly posted sign on the front. Like any good sign, there are a few elements that make it effective. It should be large enough to be noticeable, easily understood, and noted with an expected consequence if the boundaries of the fence are violated. In a real-world scenario, posted signs can say things like "Keep Out, Private Property" or "No Trespassing, Protected Area." When you see these, you immediately become aware of expectations in conduct and the desire to remain separate. While not clearly stated in typical signs of the public, there are implications of ignoring these signs and continuing past a fence or boundary. That may be a phone call to the police or a not-so-warning shot from an angry neighbor. When it comes to interpersonal boundaries, particularly those within addicted couples, not only do signs need to be posted, but they should be in bold writing with neon backgrounds. Healthy boundary signs should encompass ownership, expectation, and recourse if the fence line is crossed. If you desire to put a sign up for your boundary, make sure that it is something you can stick to, something that you are willing to follow through on, no matter the cost.

Here comes the point in treatment, and possibly in this book, when the grieved partner asks what their boundaries should be. It is a noble question and one that is made with great concern and desire to see a difference. We will go over some examples, but know that I cannot provide exact boundaries for every circumstance. I do not live the emotional experiences of my clients, so I cannot say for certainty that I know what they can handle. Good boundaries are something that can be held by the individual with the support of others. There is a wide range of boundaries that we can use moving forward. Some things need to be in place before boundaries are made and given.

First, a boundary should be made by a grieved partner with the expectation of being kept, no matter what the addicted partner says or does. If you are the grieved partner reading this and are trying to make a healthy boundary, but do not think you can stick to what you are asking, that is not a boundary. That is an ultimatum, and they do not work. You will further drive the both of you into a terrible relational dynamic that makes you both feel crazy. Forgive my abrupt wording, but I have seen too many cases where the grieved partner becomes so ready to have their voice heard that they start speaking without acknowledging and taking care of their own needs. If you are not sure what your boundaries and expectations are for the addicted partner, that is okay. Do not rush this. You are allowed to take time and consider what you would like to see happen before speaking. There is no reason to be hurried beyond what you can handle.

Next, boundaries should be vetted and supported by those that are willing to see you get better. For instance, if you are considering leaving if a relapse occurs, then make sure that a friend or family member is ready to take you the moment you realize it has happened. If there is a consideration for divorce, make sure you have spoken to whomever you need to about it before moving forward. This can be a lawyer, friend, family member, therapist, or even a spiritual mentor. Whomever you choose should be able to remain calm and understand the plan of escape if a boundary is crossed and intervention is needed.

The last aspect required for a healthy boundary is the calm and collected nature in the explanation and utilization. If a mother were to create a boundary that required her son to stay sober to continue living at home, then her crying and consolation should be handled mostly outside of a conversation with her son. She is allowed to feel sad and vulnerable about the explanation, but not the implementation. If her son were to hear the boundary, understand the need for it, and then break through, his mother has every right to solemnly kick him out of the home without further explanation. In fact, many family members and loved ones have experienced this odd feeling in their own journey. With the triangulation and mitigating factors pushed to the side, grieved partners and family members of addicts can breathe a sigh of relief knowing they did all they could.

There are some tangible boundaries to be found here. I will give some ideas and a formula for how to carry them out. All of these should be connected to healthy goals and needs in your life, not a way to get back at them for all those years of hurt. If you are the grieved partner and your addicted partner is in treatment, then preparing boundaries before discharge will give you the best results. If they are not in treatment and in active addiction, create these boundaries for yourself as you feel comfortable, but do not delay for your own sake. If the addicted partner has been sober for some time and you still feel the need for boundaries, then be assured you can make new ones as you feel are necessary. To start, your boundaries should be clear and with a specific goal in mind. This goal does not have to be immediate but should be achievable. Using the three elements of fencing, we can create boundaries like these:

I am someone who needs a healthy relationship focused on growth. I want to live honestly in my life. I am tired of being used to take care of someone who does not want to get better. If you want to stay in a relationship with me, you will not have a single drop of alcohol. If you do, we will have an emergency meeting with our therapist to discuss a plan. If you are not willing to do that or follow the plan, I will file for divorce and not look back.

I have spent years losing myself and wondering when it will be my turn to feel pain and concern. Instead, I have sacrificed so much that I do not know who I am anymore. You have gotten sober and that is great, but we are still missing something. I need you to get the help you need to figure out your emotions with a therapist or support group. If you do not, then I will start looking for a new apartment and move out by the end of the month.

I am done being used for money and a place to stay. I am your parent, not your hotel manager. Your mother and I have tried for so long to help you, but it has not worked. We feel like we have failed you. When you leave treatment, you will have to move to a sober living home. You are not allowed to walk into our home until we feel comfortable with the progress you have made in your treatment and recovery. If you do not stay in a sober living home and are kicked out, you cannot come to our home, even for a short time.

Some of these may seem harsh, and they are. To the addicted partner reading this, hearing your loved ones draw such distinct boundaries can seem demeaning. Even more, many addicts report feeling extremely shameful when they get sober and would prefer compassionate responses from their families. There are a couple of points here that can frame this well. The first is that you have taken advantage of the relationship for a long time and blurred boundaries, pushing them to do things they never imagined they were capable of. The second is that honestly, they need some space from you, even if that is just in an emotional sense. They have felt overwhelmingly required to dote on your every need and impulse for a long time. They need a break to understand themselves and what they can do in their relationship with you. This is a time for them to place their feet on the ground and have influence in the relationship. Infidelity work is very important to this process and establishing boundaries like these is necessary to retain some balanced connection.

With these explanations and examples, I will give you a blank template you can use for your boundaries with some explanations on them. Be assured that if you can make peace with yourself, your family, and your god about these boundaries, then I cannot argue with you about their necessity or implementation. They do not have to be in order or perfect and can even be written out if needed.

Using our fence post: I am someone who values ..., I want to be a person that can..., I hope that my relationships are..., My job as a parent makes me consider..., My personal beliefs would encourage me to...

Building with our boards: Because of those things, I expect..., Having said that, I have spoken to a therapist and friends and require that..., With the children in mind, I expect you to attend..., To be the best version of myself and us as a couple, we will...

Finally, our sign: If you do not engage in these things, I will be forced to..., Failing to engage in these tasks will cause me to..., If you do not take your recovery and our relationship seriously enough to do what I am asking, without regret or shame, I will follow through with my plan of....

To the grieved partner reading this template for boundaries, it can seem rather harsh to just make a demand or expectations.

Stepping outside of pure addiction territory, boundaries are a part of normal healthy interaction. If you want a closed relationship and your partner wants an open one, there are different boundaries, and you have permission to leave. Even within families, a parent can expect that an adult child will come to the house every week, and the child may refuse. If they disagree and no resolution can be made, distance can be readily formed in the relationship. In any healthy dynamic, we must understand our own boundaries, recognize the other person's boundaries, and decide how much we will engage. The use of boundaries as I described may feel wrong, but they are not. It is likely that you are so used to not having boundaries and expectations to have your own needs met, that using them now seems foreign. That is okay! This comes in time and is a useful skill in all areas of your life, including home, romance, school, and even employment. We are going to talk about why these boundaries are important and what we can do about them in a healthy relationship, but I would encourage you that aside from something criminal or strictly immoral, nearly everything is up for discussion in the creation of boundaries. If the addicted partner does not like the boundary, they are just as permitted to leave the relationship as you are.

HEALTHY DYNAMICS

Creating and maintaining a healthy relationship is tedious and life-long work. Many couples never attempt to achieve an engaging and vulnerable connection. Some can go their entire lives without being truly open and connected to their partner in every aspect of their lives. This is sad and incredibly common. I may be somewhat radical here, but I would hope that every couple could reach a point of total interconnection, understanding and knowing one another, while still maintaining their individual identity. Much like keeping a bicycle moving and providing continual maintenance, a healthy relationship will need constant care and continual exercise.

If it is difficult for most people to obtain such a lofty goal, then what hope does a couple in crisis have? How could someone in a years-long strain come to a point of vulnerability with their partner? To figure out what this could even look like, we need to understand what a healthy relationship is. They come in all shapes and sizes, but some basic building blocks are necessary for any positive and challenging relationship. The framework that will help us define comes mainly from tenants of Emotionally Focused Therapy. EFT is a wonderful extension of Attachment Theory and other systemic theories. There are some basic assumptions about what a healthy relationship is, what can keep people together and wanting to continue living with one another. Early on in EFT, there is a focus on understanding, expressing, and receiving emotional information. Each person is asked to openly express their experiences, gain support, and engage in their partner's expression as well. Once each one can understand their experiences and connect with the other, comes the next important step.

From this basis, couples are asked to turn to one another and share their pain beyond just emotions. They can articulate what is happening at the moment but must learn to have continued interaction around what is hurting them. After they can talk about the pain they are experiencing, empathy begins to set in. Barriers of frustration and disconnection start to break down and allow each member the ability to start to see the other person. For maybe the first time in a long time, each person can truly see that the partner they hoped for is on the other side.

Pain is expressed through communication, letters, interactions, conversation, and body language. As partners grow closer together, deeper hurts from the relationship and the past come up. Explanations start to become available that shed light on behavioral patterns in an individual's life and relationship dynamics. Little is done from an apology at this point. Couples describe the desire to be "held" by their partner at this point in therapy. There have likely been hundreds of apologies, but no one actually feels better. Once each person can see the depths of pain in their partner and come alongside them, a new opportunity is offered. Not only can there be a discussion of problems, but emotional resolutions are possible as well. After all, no one really believes that they can argue their partner into deep connection and vulnerability. The emotional, almost spiritual, aspect of the relationship is what brings healing.

When clients can engage in this conversation freely outside of sessions, they begin to create a new relationship based on their ability to see and know the other person for who they are. This new relationship is solidified by continual work. At this point, many therapists will describe the couple's progress by reporting that they are entering the "maintenance phase" of treatment, only needing to continue what they have been doing. I hope this is somewhat of a misnomer if it is delivered this way. Just because a bike is moving quickly, does not mean that coasting is an option. There is always the possibility of returning to old behaviors if one partner decides to opt out of the new dynamic and the other partner allows it.

Some major things to take from EFT in the realm of addiction treatment is the necessity of vulnerability, accountability, balance, and continual engagement. Vulnerability is not just being open about feelings; it is the allowance for a partner to come and sit in the pain as well. It is the hope that when they are exposed and hurting, their partner will be there to walk with them instead of rejecting them or attempting to ignore the issue. Vulnerability also requires true feedback from a partner. If someone can feel welcomed in interaction and able to receive constructive criticism, a balance begins to form. Requests can be made without fear of breakdown. A connection can be made in open communication with the ability to be accepted and asked to change.

Accountability is a huge part of EFT literature, even if it is not explicitly stated. Not only can a partner share their feelings, but they can share what they do not appreciate from the other partner and request a different relationship. This form of accountability is not one-sided. There are opportunities for each member of a couple to recognize issues and point towards cooperative solutions. Each can keep the other on the track they set out on, focusing on the goal of a better relationship.

Balance is another key factor in EFT. From the beginning of the treatment process, members of the couple are oriented away from triangulation and pushed into each other. The hope is that once couples can join against their problematic cycles of behavior and the "me against them" mentality, the connection can breed genuine change. Infidelity work naturally implements specific things that will help balance an overall relationship, like social media monitoring or phone calls throughout the day. The end result should still be a total balance that is unique and acceptable for the couple.

The last part of EFT that is important for our uses in addiction treatment is the continual effort to create a growing relationship. Just like in a sober couple, progress can be lost over time if the relational bicycle loses momentum and does not receive any more work, causing the need for a kickstand again. There is no "arrival" in a healthy relationship, where one or both members can cease learning about the other person and experiencing life with them.

Now we can look at how all of this works for addiction specifically. EFT is possibly the most effective treatment for couples and provides insight for couples in addiction as well. There are certainly complications to consider in addicted couples. First is the great intensity that couples in addiction present with. It is no secret that addiction is traumatic and affects everyone within a system, particularly a significant other. As we spoke about previously, addicted couples mistake intensity for intimacy. Unfortunately, great moments of emotion do not equal a healthy and engaged relationship. It can be tempting to think that endeavors of sobriety bring couples together emotionally, but they often do not. Without actual intimacy, vulnerability, and acceptance of the other person, unhealthy cycles can continue.

Another great concern for couples in addiction is the drastic differences experienced by the grieved partner when they look at the addicted partner. Before addiction, there can be one version of an addict that then shifts when active addiction comes into play and another when they first enter sobriety. In typical couple relationships, there are general drifts and sometimes more radical changes, but nothing as stark as the addict in the middle of using. In a healthy long-term relationship, there is continued growth in the relationship. How do you build a relationship with someone who has been three different people? Something important to hear for each member of a couple is that in the middle of addiction and the early stages of recovery, neither one of you recognizes yourself and you have no idea who the other person is. Triangulation has torn true vulnerability away and a rotted sense of self-identity remains. There is no way to have a healthy recovery in the emotional state where each member is amid active addiction.

In many cases of a couple's work, therapists will look back to better memories, often when couples met and first became exclusive in their relationship. There are usually good times that are pure in experience to look back to when things become difficult. Unfortunately, addiction may taint these memories when the truth comes out around the timelines of addiction and the grieved partner realizes just how far back patterns of addiction have gone. Because of this possible barrier, it is often the case that an entirely new relationship is needed for a couple. Certainly, there are elements of each person that are kept, and memories that are shared. However, doubt has likely been cast over the entire relationship, making it difficult to ground in the past.

In EFT, there is a large emphasis on understanding the dynamics of arguments and how they are sustained. There is an investigation into triggers and moments that increase problematic interactions. For the couple in addiction, these triggers can be grand and incredibly small. Some triggers are unique for each partner, sometimes unrecognized and misunderstood. Some of the practical triggers that affect the grieved partner I have seen are the cracking of a soda can related to drinking alcohol in the past, sniffling related to past cocaine use, tiredness due to the effect of opiates, distraction due to marijuana use, and even misunderstanding of a comment due to any number of intoxicants. Some practical triggers for the addicted partner I have seen are being asked "Are you okay?" to probe for sobriety, rolling eyes from mistrust of sobriety, yelling from frustration in relationship progress, and even slamming a car door as a threat of leaving. Some of these things are innocent in isolation. There is nothing inherently concerning about sniffling or having someone ask how you are doing today. As was discussed in the chapter on trauma, there are little things that would warn us of coming danger in the middle of addiction that we can look for in recovery as well. We do not want to nitpick in couples therapy, but recognizing these small triggers that lead to greater arguments can give us great insight into the interactional cycles in addiction and recovery.

With all of this information given to the couple, I will now speak directly to the grieved partner. I do not want to ignore the addicted partner, but I have seen great strides in helping the addict in recovery and little support for the partner that was also in the middle of the entire process. Starting with the harsher perspectives, grieved partners will also have unhealthy coping skills. Whether someone argues that their unhealthy coping comes from their partner's addiction is irrelevant. Not addressing your own issues does not allow for growth for either one of you. If something terrible were to happen, the addicted partner would leave or die, then all you would be left with is unhealthy coping that cannot be blamed on anyone. In extreme versions of this, there are scenarios where grieved partners have their underlying addiction that is hidden underneath the great catastrophe of their addicted partner. Dad may have a problem with whiskey and drunk driving, but mom may also have a problem with Xanax and chardonnay. Her use is more "controlled," so it is less likely to be seen by the family and required to be addressed.

If the addicted partner comes to a full sense of healing, anything harmful you hold onto will also come to light. Many grieved partners become resentful of a request to give up their own vices. They have become a way for the grieved partner to have their sense of escape away from the addicted partner. Remember, codependency requires two people. It requires a dissolution of healthy boundaries and positive coping. If the addicted partner is to find healing in the relationship, you have to acknowledge your role in what has happened as well. Sure, you probably do not provide al-

cohol for their bedside table in the morning and may have no idea
where to even find street drugs, but you have played your own part
in this relationship.

The key to accepting your role in addiction often comes not
from what you have endorsed or supported, but from what you
tolerated and accepted. This is often the key to addiction within
a couple. Many grieved partners will say that they hate their partner's addiction and pray every day for it to be over. Somehow, after
years of wanting it to be over, you have stayed. For something so
terrible to you and the relationship, you are still there. You cannot
hate it as much as you espouse or demand that it be over with. If
you were really not okay with it, the relationship would have ended a long time ago. Over time, you made small compromises, small
adjustments to your fence line that you do not recognize just how
far you have given up on yourself. By the time you are reading this,
you probably have no idea where your posts are, boards have been
hastily thrown together and signs are sloppy handwriting on post-
it notes. The bare minimum of your contribution to addiction is
making a long string of compromises that have allowed the addicted partner to slip and allowed you to not address your own issues
and hold to your own standards.

On a more positive note, I have seen both in research and in
my practice that grieved partners have the greatest influence on an
addicted partner's recovery. In both a positive and negative sense,
long-term committed partners can effectively sway an addict towards recovery or relapse. I have seen outcomes of a wife bringing
her husband alcohol while he was in the parking lot of a treatment
center, a husband refusing to acknowledge problems that caused
further struggle, and a girlfriend holding her ground to leave if her
boyfriend refuses treatment and therapy. The number one indica-
tor of relapse in addiction is not liquor stores, addicted friends, or
even the ability to receive certain types of treatment. It is family
stress. It is how those closest to the addict cope with changes and
how much hope they still have for the future. What this means is,
as the grieved partner, you have the greatest impact on what happens next. You do not have absolute control and may not even have

majority influence. Still, outside of the addicted partner's process of healing and willingness to work on their issues, you are the single greatest factor in this effort of recovery.

If you are willing to take the step to make your voice heard in the relationship, there are a few things to consider. First, you have to decide whether you want to stay in this relationship or not. There have been cases that I have seen and personally worked with where the grieved partner realized that they no longer wanted to be connected with the addicted partner. Many who have realized that they no longer want to stay come to recognize that they have only stayed to make sure that the addicted partner does not die. Once they see that the addicted partner can make it on their own, they file for divorce. It is not uncommon to hear of divorces being filed while an addict is in treatment or right after they leave. This is a valid response that comes from years of staying for the benefit of the addict rather than the relationship. For grieved partners, do what you can to make peace with the transition.

For those that wish to stay in the relationship or are unsure about what they would like to do, some great things will be required of you. You will have to admit to allowing this to happen for so long, giving of yourself and possibly damaging your children. You will also have to acknowledge your tendency to force the addict into their old role, even if they are working towards recovery. The grieved partner has learned to wear trauma and chaos like a warm blanket. It will take a significant amount of time to come from underneath that terrible cycle you have come to find comfort in. There is also a great deal of work that you will have to engage in. The addict will have to find a new sense of safety and grounding and so will you. There is a whole new life for you to find as well.

If you have read this far and still wish to give the relationship a shot, here is a guide for what you can do next. Acknowledge your needs and address the underlying feelings of an emotional affair. Connect with people who are knowledgeable about addiction and recovery to find balance and support. Come up with a plan that aligns with your boundaries. Make sure it allows for space for both of you to grow over time. Be clear about expectations and most importantly, if you say you will leave if you find that they have relapsed, leave. I tell clients in this situation that after years of compromise and struggle, they can leave whenever they choose. There have been years of not tending to their own needs. What may be considered selfish could be required to rebalance the relationship. Aside from any religious or personal beliefs, there is no obligation to stay. The addicted partner is not a child. They are not incapable. They should not be treated as an invalid.

I will end this chapter with something that has helped many clients and couples in treatment, a statement about the need a grieved partner has with expectations for the future. You can modify this however you like, but something similar can provide the needed clarity for the next steps in a relationship.

"I acknowledge and take responsibility for my role in your addiction. I have made years of compromises in my soul and the health of our relationship. I did not leave when I said I would or follow through on what I said was required. For that, I allowed our relationship to fall apart. However, I do not take responsibility for your addiction or how it has impacted us. I do not apologize for your addiction, but I do apologize for creating an environment where your addiction was tolerated and grown. I am taking a journey towards health. I am inviting you to join me on this journey. If you do not, I will go without you and find a better version of myself. I request that you do what I have asked of you for your health and our relationship. I hope one day we can find a new life together that is better than we ever had."

GROWING THE SKYLARK'S FEATHERS BACK

MUCH OF WHAT has been discussed in this book thus far can feel somewhat discouraging. It can feel overwhelming to take in such a large amount of information and the possible weight of what has happened over the years. Some may even feel burdened by what they have learned. Take heart and a breath before continuing. You will need it. There is much more to read and far more to do in your life.

At this point in the book, we are turning to a more constructive approach to addiction. More information will be given about the dynamics of addiction, but restorative ideas and processes will come to light. I hope that you can take these things in and see that there is a path for the future.

ADDICTION CYCLE

Addiction and the effects of it are traumatic and can seem random. The ways in which we are affected as addicts or as someone close to them can be unpredictable with the complexity of what defines use. Here, we will go over what the addiction cycle generally is so that everyone is on the same page. Most people with experience in addiction or recovery have heard this. For those that have not, this cycle is used to give insight into what happens around the use of substances and how one thing can lead to another. The order of this cycle is trigger, craving, ritual, use, and guilt.

The first part of the cycle is the trigger. This is a word that is overused in today's society. If everything is a trigger, there are no triggers. It is just life and life sucks sometimes. A true definition of a trigger is an outside force that sparks an unhealthy or traumatic response. Triggers can be good or bad. The smell of cookies triggers a warm and happy feeling in me. The sound of Christmas music triggers a nauseating, visceral response. The outside world gives us input on what is happening and what we can expect.

Addiction triggers are outside actions or responses that bring a sense of anxiety, dread, or fear related to the addicted person's past. These can be anything from a discarded plastic bag, someone constantly sniffling, to the opening of a soda can. These immediate triggers are directly related to the use of substances themselves. With some effort, these triggers are easy to spot, predict, and possibly avoid. Someone in recovery can take a different drive home to avoid a liquor store or stop interacting with individuals that still use substances. If the opening of a can is a concern to someone, then only buying bottles of soda and water could be an easy fix.

Other triggers could be considered secondary or things that are a step away from using itself. These could be counting dollar bills in their pocket, knowing a drug test will be coming from work, or someone asking if they feel "okay." These tend to be a bit more difficult to spot, with specific knowledge that is needed to address individual concerns. Triggers such as these also are either harder to recognize at the moment for an addict, but easier to hide as well. A concerned wife can instinctively know that having liquor around is a trigger for her husband. She may not realize that doing spring cleaning may also trigger a response from her husband where he relives a past trauma of watching her frantically find the bottle he hid.

The last set of triggers I will mention is more fluid in nature.

These hidden triggers are connected to reminders of past traumas, past harmful interactions, or emotions that are too overwhelming to process at the moment. The most elusive of the three, hidden triggers are the most difficult to spot and name, even for therapists. Some examples of these could include a phone call from a number with a familiar area code, seeing a car similar to the one that was used as a temporary home, or a boyfriend that is being "abnormally" quiet that day. With the assumptions that are built into these triggers, it can be difficult for anyone to manage. No one can predict who will call, there is no way to control who is on the road, and someone having a bad day is their right to process however they please.

Following the trigger in the addiction cycle is craving. Both physiological and psychological in nature, a craving is a desire to fill in the gap someone feels due to withdrawals from substances or the hole of desperation that is ever-present. Cravings may come about immediately after a trigger arises or may build up over time. This ramp-up is normal for someone in all stages of addiction and recovery. What may start as a twinge of desire can jump to a full-on ravenous hunt for the next ability to use. While not a concrete rule, there can be some consideration for the severity of someone's addictive cycles with a proper understanding of how long someone moves from a trigger to developed craving. Those with little tolerance for the emotional strain can easily find themselves needing to use it directly after a trigger.

Someone's body can show physical responses to cravings. "The shakes" and racing thoughts are commonly reported symptoms of cravings or the need to use. Even without an outside trigger, the lowered dopamine and level of someone's drug of choice can bring about a biological trigger, starting the addiction cycle over again. Panic can also ensue with craving, showing through a rise in heart rate and adrenaline, which triggers the survival response that has been wired towards addiction by now.

There are also social and attachment-related levels of craving as well. Before, I gave information about how addiction is not purely biological because an active addict can feel lowered levels of withdrawal and panic if they know that their drug of choice is either on the way or they are on their way to get it. The panic that spiked the heart rate and the shaking that came from lack of use can easily dissipate, even without using any drugs or alcohol at all. It is also worth mentioning that cravings can be intense when trying to resist them initially, but seem less ominous if the addict has resolved to use and has started a plan to follow through.

The next step in the cycle is the ritual. Typically, addicts have a routine that they use to get and use their drug of choice. The cocaine addict will give the same message to the same dealer and meet them in the same place. The alcoholic will go to the same liquor store they go to on Thursdays so that they can get exactly what they need. In healthy individuals, rituals are a helpful way to remain grounded and have reasonable expectations for what can happen next. For those in active addiction, rituals are a way to enforce guardrails to keep their head afloat.

Rituals can vary to some degree. Someone who is attempting to hide their addiction may have a few places where they drink or use. They could even have a few different hiding places and excuses they could use if someone were to find them out. Rituals can be either literal actions that someone goes through or can be mental gymnastics to rationalize their use. Some of these mental rituals can be a distance they create between themselves, their use, and the connections they have with the ones they love. However, this works for the individual addict, the presence of a ritual signals the nearly inevitable next step.

Using the substance itself is what follows. This takes little explanation for anyone to grasp. Whether it be a drink, a bump, a pill, or a needle, the process of using is the follow-through on everything that has built up. This is the culmination of shame that has become so unbearable that it seems as if use is the only thing to soothe the beast that has become menacing and overgrown. The only thing left to say is that this point is the pinnacle of the Addiction Cycle and what will be the repeated result after some time.

The final measure in this swan song is called guilt. I disagree with this labeling. While it makes sense to call the horrid feelings someone has after using guilt, I believe it goes much deeper. I can feel guilty about eating too much for Thanksgiving or for speaking harshly to someone. This form of guilt is more akin to an inner recognition of the need to change. I would argue that guilt is a necessary part of the human experience. We should feel guilty if we harm someone or take advantage of a situation. Instead, I would label the final step in the addiction cycle as shame.

Shame, this deep feeling of a flawed self that cannot be changed drives the next steps in the cycle. In this, addicts may promise to never use again if they were caught. At the time, there may be an intense interaction in which you may wish you could believe them. Sadly, the repeated interactions with shame have caused a lack of belief and engagement. While legitimate and healthy to be suspicious of intentions, the addict can be further driven into shame.

During this experience of shame comes a desire to hide evidence and put away things that could expose just how bad things have gotten. Some addicts may even admit to smaller amounts of usage, just to deflect from larger amounts that could concern people. This shame also drives individuals towards isolation and quick resolution. Addicts can make promises and even make small "improvements" that fall away once the cycle repeats.

A cloud of shame will then linger until the next trigger. For some, the intense feelings of shame are enough to start the cycle over again. After the drugs or alcohol wear off, emotions start to come back. Once those come back and they recognize just how badly they have screwed their life up, the cycle can start again. Deep scars and negative beliefs about themselves keep addicts within the cycle. Without hope for themselves, change, or the future, they remain trapped until they get yanked out by someone or they die.

FAMILY RECOVERY CYCLE

When someone is admitted to treatment, family members or significant others are often allowed to become involved in the process of recovery and discharge. Some facilities will provide counseling and others will just give general updates. Whether it is to these or something else, it is typical for families to feel as if there is a lack of information. This disconnection from experience comes partially due to the nature of addiction, but also from a lack of knowledge and support in their own experience. When family members and loved ones are given information about addiction, it often mirrors what addicts are taught in rehab. Little is given about their relationship with their loved one's use or how they can go through cycles of emotion and responding to addiction.

What is given to families and loved ones can feel as if it is against them. Avoiding triggers can easily be misconstrued as an excuse for the addict to not be challenged in beliefs and expectations. Getting support through community groups or sponsorships can leave family members feeling as if they are passive members in recovery and do not have a place to speak up. This is incredibly tragic for me as a Marriage and Family Therapist. Unfortunately, there is little overlap between my area of counseling and addiction literature. So, I ask that you take this next bit of information as worthwhile as it could help explain what family members go through in the process of addiction.

Those close to someone in active addiction feel their sense of trauma. This was discussed earlier. They give responses from a place of fear and concern. Instead of exploring that, I would like to give you the overall cycle that I have seen families go through in the process of addiction and attempts at recovery. I will speak of these stages with the assumption that a rehabilitation facility or some level of treatment is on the horizon. The cycle generally works in this order: Going In, Going Out, Going Down, and Going on. The first part of the cycle comes from the decision that something has to change. After riding the roller coaster for long enough, it is finally time to do something about it. This is characterized by the feeling of having nothing else to do or that there is a last straw in the relationship.

Going In is initiated in a few different ways. The first way that this stage begins is through a boundary, ultimatum, or thinly veiled threat. I spoke about the difference between a boundary and an ultimatum before, but this is where it can come into play practically and how it will enact long-term results. I added a thinly veiled threat here to emphasize the fervent and desperate nature of dealing with an addict. An ultimatum can feel like a large demonstration of desperation, and a thinly veiled threat is an off comment that can end up sparking the voicing of larger needs.

Once the realization of consequences comes in, there is a process of intake. If someone is medically fragile due to their use, then a hospital stay may be required before admission to a drug and alcohol facility. Once interventions are completed and someone is finally admitted, some curious things happen for loved ones. First, there can be a mix of guilt and intense relief. Many families speak about their ability to sleep well for the first time in a long time. Knowing that their loved one is at least sober and safe can make a huge difference. Also, this can also be true if someone is arrested for drug use, that is assuming that there is no access to drugs when they are incarcerated.

Many loved ones will report that their body relaxes or collapses once the addict is admitted and kept for a stay in treatment. If you are currently in this situation, I would urge you to take time to be mindful of your body. You may have been ignoring your aches and pains, or you may have tension and stress in muscles you did not realize before. Some may realize that they are actually hungry or need a nap. Partially due to trauma, but also due to concern for their loved ones, family members can neglect themselves and their relationships.

Once everything is settled and a good night's sleep is under the belt comes another aspect of Going In. If you are newer to the recovery world, you may have what is called magical thinking. I am not saying you believe in pixie dust that makes you fly. What I do mean is a deep need to believe that everything is going to be okay. Considering all the tragedy that has come about and the wake of destruction that has followed your addicted loved one, hope for miracles can be all that is left. Much like everything else talked about in this book, this is normal. We hope that our husband can finally get it and be the father he needs to be. We wish our mother would see the need to change and turn her life around. Our blind hope keeps us from seeing the reality of the struggle everyone is about to go through. For those that are unwilling veterans of the recovery journey, our hope can look much more like apathy. A desire for life to be different has all but dissipated and we become numb to the process altogether.

Just as we catch our breath and realize that our loved one is safe, we are hit with the next phase in the cycle, Going Out. You get a call about the impending discharge. Whether it was due to insurance denial, a recent concern, or a planned discharge date that seemingly came too quickly, the time is up for rest and real life is about to hit again. The process of Going Out includes both the planning to leave, as well as the initial process of return, and it is finally here.

Some loved ones experience panic and either freeze up and take no clinical recommendations or panic and make sure their loved one leaves with appointments for every possible type of provider. Many will describe that phone call as a thrust back into everything that was left behind upon their admission. All the memories and fears come back. From this comes both bracing for impact as well as possible extreme magical thinking. In this stage of the recovery process, we can wish that everything would work and they could come out of treatment completely healed. This is sweet but incredibly ignorant. I do not mean that in a harsh way, but as an abrupt jolt to help you realize that when someone leaves treatment, not much has changed. The only thing that can be guaranteed is that they are not in any physical danger of withdrawals and have no direct biological reason to use again. Every ounce of shame and fear they went in with is still there, and now they do not even get to drink to deal with it.

Again, I say this for your benefit. Many addicts will play off this obliviousness either through their internal ignorance or in the ability to manipulate those around them. In the best-case scenario, an addict will engage in magical thinking because that is all they can believe about themselves. They have screwed up so much that the only chance in life is for a miracle to happen. If I were cynical about it, addicts use this thinking to create assurance that their actions are virtuous. For instance, they miss meetings because they are enjoying life and the newfound freedom they have, and definitely not because they are avoiding accountability and drinking on the side.

You should feel ashamed for keeping them at the word that they promised on their parents' graves! If you just left them alone in their newly blossoming life and journey, all would be well! Give me a break.

Anxiety is a descriptor in all aspects of recovery, particularly in Going Out. This anxiety can morph into the ways that we treat our significant other. We can desire to take their word for their continued sobriety. We can want to believe that things are better. So, in an effort to not trigger their addiction and see if things are okay, we start asking roundabout questions. Some of these include, "How are you feeling today," or "What is your plan for the day?" Certainly not limited to those two options, I think you get the idea. Loved ones will pry just enough to make themselves feel assured about progress, but only end up increasing their anxiety by not getting straightforward answers.

The last part of Going Out is another personal soapbox of mine. So, if you are not used to my rants at this point, you either are a glutton for punishment or somehow see hope in what you are reading. I hope it's the latter, but I can settle for the former. Either through direct conversation with the addict in treatment or through implication in speaking with members of a clinical team, family members and loved ones can feel as if they have to treat the person leaving rehab with little kid gloves. This is also described as walking on eggshells. Somehow, the idea comes about that the entire process of recovery can fall apart with one wrong conversation or comment. So, family members and loved ones will engage in prejudicial low expectations, not requiring significant work or accountability from the addict. Let me be clear. If the person going into treatment is an adult, then treat them like one. If they need to get a job to help pay for things, then they need to get a job to help pay for things. If you need help taking care of the children by driving them places or helping with dinner, they should help. Then they should be expected to help with that in all other relevant areas as well. Do not handicap someone's ability to recover by not allowing them to grow up. Sure, all things need to be given in time and grace should be extended in their effort to reintegrate into the family, but a significant portion of recovery is taking responsibility for what is required, and this is your chance to ask that of them.

Once time has passed and things have settled down, Going Down starts to creep in. This phase is characterized by the feeling that not much has changed. Sure, the drinking or using is gone, but all of the same emotions and fears are still present. If you are the family member in this case, it can feel as if you are concerned that they are still using, even though they are doing everything correctly and have no way to use. This can be the same for everyone involved. Here is where the term "dry drunk" comes into play. A dry drunk is someone who is sober but has not developed the skills necessary to cope with the emotional strain that comes with recovery. They become miserable in their own life and miserable to be around.

One thing that is common for couples is to feel happy but unhappy. Sure, everything that was required for discharge is met, but life is not as it should be. Do not get me wrong, you got everything you asked for. She is sober, healthy, and working towards her goals in life. Still, something is missing. You can even feel distant due to seeing her sober but still feel as if she is in some far away emotional country. There is something important to remember here. If someone's only goal is to be sober, then they will ultimately fail. Honestly, sobriety is a stupid and expensive goal all on its own. Technically, with enough zip ties, anyone can be made to get sober and it will not cost insurance a dime. Sobriety is a first step, but cannot be the end goal.

The lack of connection in this part of the cycle starts to bring a few things to the surface. The addict can find themselves considering relapse due to the dejectedness and lack of success that they feel in their relationships. They can view life as predictably miserable whether they are sober or not, but at least when they were using, they did not feel it as much. Going Down can also produce fights in couples and families that lead to great arguments. Usually, this is due to underlying emotions and issues starting to become more realized. If you spent ten years holding your tongue about your pain and fear during your husband's use, he might be sober enough to hear about it now. If you drank for the past five years to hold down your overwhelming shame of failure as a father, that may become a point of contention in the relationship.

As a therapist who specializes in working with couples in addiction and recovery, I usually get a call to start therapy in the midst of Going Down. Everything that was completed was supposed to make the relationship better, but it did not. Instead, counseling becomes a last resort to hopefully make sense of why there is still significant distrust and animosity towards one another, even when every drug test is clean, medications are being taken, and meeting attendance is perfect. This is jarring enough for both members of a couple. Neither feels better about their relationship, but they got everything they begged for and asked for.

At this point, it becomes apparent that the spouse of the addict only asked for sobriety because they did not hold any significant belief that a true relationship was possible. After years of disaster, sobriety seemed like the only thing that could be accomplished. That is difficult enough on its own. The addict in recovery may also only seek sobriety to achieve some sort of goal to get a trophy to show off. From a more cynical perspective, addicts can push for sobriety to relieve pressure from loved ones about the need to change their life. Either way, underlying issues continue to arise, and relationships become nearly unbearable.

The final stage is Going On. Here is where major decisions are made. These resolutions are often more concrete than in previous stages. When family members and loved ones are in the Going On part of the cycle, they are deciding whether or not they will continue in the craziness of relapse and promises of sobriety, or decide to cut ties. If a relapse is a reality, then Going On looks like a further integration into the struggle or leaving altogether. Either one of these is valid, but one is more difficult than the other. This continued engagement in the Addiction Cycle and repeat of the Family Recovery Cycle will do one thing for sure. It will take more of your soul with it. Some people continue to give of themselves to support their addicted loved ones out of fear or trauma of previous losses. Some have resolved to make this attempt at recovery the last shot. Those that make those resolutions are often able to be coerced into full investment into the addict's lifestyle when shame is leveraged and ultimatums are seen through.

Even if the addict stays completely sober, Going On can still take effect. This often comes from a realization that the person they were hoping to rediscover is no longer there. Parents can push through years of struggle to find their little boy back, only to find that he is not on the other end of this journey. A wife may yearn for the love that she used to share with her husband, only to see a shell of a man she does not recognize. With directionless desperation, family members and loved ones can search for something to make sense of their journey. If they do not find it, they may decide to finally walk away. They may only be able to vocalize that they have no idea where their loved one went, and that alcohol must have stolen them away long ago.

Resolution of divorce, disconnection, or persistent apathy sets in. Everyone has become numb to the process, honestly unable to feel disappointed by relapse or happy about accomplishments. So, with every checkbox accounted for, every doctor's appointment attended, and every recommendation taken, wives will leave. Husbands can see their wives sober for three years and decide to finally divorce. Their flame of hope has finally been quenched, and they cannot care anymore. While incredibly disheartening to see as a therapist who tries to have hope for every addict, I do get it. I do not blame family members or loved ones for feeling so exhausted by the constant process of addiction, recovery, and relapse that they quit. There are true cases where family members have nothing left to give. Sometimes that drive can come back and sometimes it does not.

IMPORTANT FACTORS

If you read those two cycles and can identify either yourself or someone you care about, there are some things you need to consider. First, today's recovery world is not what it has been in years past. In some circles, relapse is seen as a part of the process of recovery. I do not pretend to be so gracious or considerate. This is not due to a hateful view of recovery or the struggle that it represents, but the implication that comes from an allowance from use. An addict may be able to rationalize that relapse can be a part of their journey, but family members and loved ones may not have that same luxury. Each relapse may be the last one family members can bear to see someone deal with.

It can be grounding to understand the cycles of addiction and family recovery. However, the presence of an overdose can bring everything to a full stop. A relapse, even on something like cocaine or pills may have more than someone bargained for. Due to the influx of Fentanyl, my fears of the consequences of relapse have increased. If someone is not aware of the presence of this potent drug in what they are ingesting, they can immediately die from an opioid overdose. Even if someone intentionally ingests this drug, it could be the last time they do it. Drug dealers are not known for their consistency and adherence to FDA regulations. If this seems odd to you, there are many celebrities over the years that have fallen prey to a misdistribution of substances.

I do not want to use the graves of dead celebrities to drive my point home, but a short search of celebrity overdoses online will show a grim pattern. Some have taken drugs past a recommended amount and overdosed, and some unknowingly ingested a lethal amount of a substance their body was not accustomed to. If all of these celebrities died due to overdose, I am not sure why the common person would have great confidence that what they put into their bodies is untainted by something other than what they paid for. Those in high influence surely pay top dollar for their drugs and their dealers are aware of whom they are selling to. If all of those expectations and checkpoints are not enough to stop an accidental overdose, there is no hope for the cocaine addict to avoid a mix of drugs they did not expect.

Another important factor in this understanding of addiction cycles is the reminder that you can get off at any point in this crazy merry-go-round. I spoke about this before, but I want to drive home that someone's addiction is not your problem. If you have been on board for the crazy coaster for this long, you have done more than enough. If you are reading this as the addict in hopeful recovery, your family and loved ones do not owe you anything. They love you and want to help you, but do not abuse their mercy. Sure, some element of grace is needed for the process of recovery, and some days will be better than others. Your addiction has drained everyone around you. Healing is possible, and you can become whole, but that does not come from a spirit of entitlement that continually demands from people who have sacrificed their lives and sanity.

The last important point to make here is that while what I am sharing may be a sense of hope that many have not felt in some time, there is no guarantee that understanding and intervention in this process will assure permanent recovery. In all honesty, recovery can be a numbers game. If you were to take every bit of advice from this book and apply it to your life or the relationships that you hold, you may be taking the best chance at recovery, but not one that is assured. Even if you do everything right, an addict can still leave. If you go to every meeting and have been sober for two years, your husband can leave you. None of this information should be used as a way to cure anxiety, but to take a shot at things possibly being better. Once you have done everything you can do, have peace that you have done everything you can do. If you are not sure what that means, I tell clients that if they can make peace with themselves, their family, and their god, I cannot argue with them. I would encourage the same thinking here.

GAINING SUPPORT

For any family members or loved ones reading this, consider getting support for the road forward. If you are looking for insight on where to get off on the Family Recovery Cycle so that it does not continue, anywhere will do. If you find yourself wanting to intervene at the beginning, speak to someone knowledgeable about this and get grounded. There is no need to be thrown around by all manner of chaos involved in unhealthy recovery.

Your decision to stick through the pain should be your own. If you are willing to endure the trials of Going On to see if there is anything left in your loved one, do so mindfully. Learning about these cycles does not inoculate someone from the effects of addiction. Instead, you will be able to say that no matter what happens and what you are willing to tolerate is totally up to you. If you do wish to endure, make sure you have support from a few different kinds of people. First, you will need people who love and care for you, no matter their knowledge or experience with addiction. These friends will allow for assistance in your emotional expression, no matter what the outcome of your relationship is. You will also need people that are knowledgeable about addiction and will be able to speak the harsh truth without the filter of social grace. While abrasive at times, the truth-tellers give us a window into what could be possible in our own lives. Finally, you will need people in your life that can remain somewhat neutral but will be able to remain steadfast and courageous enough to walk recovery with you. As a guide for your journey forward, they can point out patterns and parse out the entanglement of trying to find sobriety in a new world.

Again, I will say, if you see everything in front of you and are unable to walk forward, take a moment. I encourage you to find a place or people that can hear you out. Once you come to a point of peace where you can make an informed, but lasting decision, do it. If that decision is to walk away and not look back, okay. Little advice is given to the mother who cries daily about whether her son is alive. Much is required of the boyfriend who cannot cope with the consequences of his partner's actions. If you can come to a point of peace and silence and resolve to leave, then go in peace and find healing. I am not asking you to be selfish or to make the whole situation surround your discomfort. Instead, if there is no healing to be found or no energy left to travel, honor that. The addict is given voices of hope from many places in the modern world. If this is the only place you hear it, then I hope you pay attention. You need healing too, even if they never change.

WELCOME TO THE THUNDERDOME

T HE LAST CHAPTER in this semi-organized cluster of addiction education and treatment ends with my thoughts, feelings, and topics that have been helpful in my work but do not necessarily fit in any other category. Weaving a story within education and a sense of hope is a true joy of mine. Instead of a cohesive stream of discussion, this section will contain many things that I have found helpful in my work with addiction. I apologize if some of these things seem disconnected, but they can be helpful for anyone involved with addicts, from counselors to friends, and may even help explain behaviors and beliefs that have confused even addicts themselves.

FROM THE THERAPY ROOM

This first section of ideas about addiction and recovery comes from revelations and discussions within my therapy sessions, both in groups and individual sessions. Some were brought to my attention through clients themselves, while some are the recognition of patterns that exist in addiction and recovery. None of these are 100% true in all cases, but I would bet nearly all addicts experience these things.

The intertwining of guilt and shame is an interesting dynamic in recovery. Guilt, the ability to understand that we did something wrong, is incredibly useful. We are connected through our sense of right and wrong. Whether that is due to socialization or some innate writing on our hearts, we all carry a basic understanding of what is expected of us. Shame, on the other hand, is something else entirely. Instead of saying that I did something wrong, as would be the case for guilt, shame tells us that we *are* something wrong. This message cuts to our inner being, defining us and setting a course for how we can pay penance for the rest of our lives. From this shame comes two important topics I discuss with all of my clients.

The life-debt is something lost in modern society at large. When our lives are saved, we are content with thanking the person who took the time and moving on. However, a life-debt refers to the feeling that the rest of your days must be in service to the one who saved you or took ownership of you. The addict, particularly the married one, can feel this shame and indebtedness towards their partner with the belief that they have caused so much harm that they should not make any more trouble. This is pushed to extreme levels where recovering addicts can neglect themselves and their feelings to not impose on their partner. Their shame in being has become so great, they do not want their problems to spill over. What can be seen as guarded feelings in an addict by the nonaddicted spouse may actually be an intense shame for all of the pain the addict caused their partner. So, they continue internal torture until their emotions inevitably explode.

The other form of shame that is common in addicts, especially those in early recovery, is the use of shame as a motivating factor to accomplish anything. Instead of looking toward the future for what is possible, the recovering addict uses shame to force themselves into "right" decisions. Instead of hoping for a better future, they use memories of how terrible they have been to manipulate themselves into not returning to old behavior. This skill becomes so innate that shame becomes the tool for all occasions. Even in couple's therapy, the recovering addict is so accustomed to using shame as a motivator for change, that they can become inaccessible to their partner. The shame shield protects against pain and possible relapse but also blocks out any sense of vulnerability and true connection.

Fear of the world is common for everyone in early recovery. Part of our modern world has allowed for great interconnection, but also very intense messaging and bids for attention. What was once a simple planning endeavor to avoid liquor stores on a drive home from work has become infinitely more complicated. Whether you are aware or not, drugs and alcohol have become more accessible than they have ever been. Lockdowns showed us that liquor stores are a necessity in modern culture. While restaurants and other normal outdoor activities were prohibited, liquor stores were allowed to remain open for the entirety of the pandemic, clearly marked as essential. Even more than that, there are delivery services for alcohol. Again, pushing the possibilities of connection, COVID created a hub for delivery. Need bred innovation and innovation bred home-delivered vodka on demand. Taking away the alcoholic's keys does not work anymore. Drugs are a whole other issue. For a long time, apps like Snapchat and Instagram have been used to sell drugs. The sheer volume and a veneer of anonymity has allowed Snapchat's "temporary" messaging to become a highway for drug sales. No longer does the drug addict have to go searching for the right guy at a bus stop or street corner. All it takes is $20, a smartphone, and an internet connection. We are past the times of being able to isolate someone in early recovery. We have to change our tactics.

Part of this shift also needs to come in our attitudes towards relapse with drugs of any kind. Alcohol is exempt from this need to change as its contents are usually bottled and monitored by the FDA. Unfortunately, this is not the case for pills and powders. There has always been a fear that something you get on the street could have any drug or substance in it, not just what you thought you were buying. What that typically meant in the past is getting baking soda in your cocaine or filler in your heroin. That has changed with one recent development in the drug trade I spoke about earlier: Fentanyl. Incredibly cheap, easy to make, and significantly more potent opioid than heroin, Fentanyl can be thrown into nearly anything. What can seem like legitimate pills from someone's sold prescription can be homemade pressed pills with a wide range of possible ingredients. What is scary to me as a therapist and researcher is just how often Fentanyl is put in street drugs that are not mainly comprised of opioids. It has even caught abusers of Xanax off guard, causing a shocking and unexpected overdose. It simply does not make sense anymore to attempt neutrality in relapse. Often, practitioners will say that relapse is a normal part of recovery. Unfortunately, I do not believe we have that indulgence anymore. You cannot recover from an unexpected fatal overdose. Even relapsing on Adderall from the street can be a ticking time bomb for a stray dose of Fentanyl that was snuck in by a previous pill press.

Contrary to popular belief and the chagrin of some clients, I am not in the business of fixing people. In graduate school, I was bound and determined to see every person as a puzzle I could solve if I was just smart and educated enough. That did not work out well with real clients. Instead, my goal is to move all of the obstacles out of the way so that individuals can make true choices on what they would like to do with their lives. Addiction, like all severe mental health disorders, causes a heavily weighted dichotomy. Here is an example I frequently use for clients. Imagine that you wake up in the morning and on your dresser are laid out two shirts, a red one and a blue one. Now, a typical person would look at those and make a decision based on what is happening and what they are feeling that day. Let us imagine that instead of those shirts being just red and blue, the red shirt symbolized addiction, and the blue one symbolized recovery. The typical individual would be able to see the outcomes and say that obviously, the blue shirt is the best choice. They would then move on and wonder why anyone would dare choose the red shirt. They may even shame someone for "choosing" their addictive behavior. Here is the kicker, those in active addiction see those two shirts clearly, but seem to know something that no one else does. That blue shirt has a bear trap under it that is hidden and primed to tear their hand off if they get too close.

For the addict, this changes everything. Sure, they could choose to go towards recovery, but they would be grabbing for a blue shirt that would cut their hand off and kill them. It makes more sense to keep wearing red until they can find a safer way to move forward. Working with addiction is teaching that while they are sure that they will die if they go for a blue shirt, there is nothing life-threatening there. It is teaching them that there is only the danger of discomfort and vulnerability, both of which are tolerable with time and practice. Before berating the addict in your life about choosing addiction, just know that yes, there is a choice. At this time, it is a false choice with only two wrong answers.

In my work with every client I have, but especially in those with addiction histories, I have noticed something common amongst all of them. They all lack the same thing—hope. After clearing all of the rubble, we come to a cliff. Much like Harrison Ford's leap of faith in the *Last Crusade*, a choice must be made to step out and see what happens if they jump. However, the jump of an addict in early recovery is a long way away. Being sober is a decent but ultimately pointless goal, especially when it comes to treatment. If all someone wants is to be sober, they need those zip ties I talked about earlier and a good buddy to spoon-feed them for a week. You technically do not need treatment to get sober. You do not need it to stay that way. It sure doesn't hurt though. This task to find hope to jump is perilous for many addicts and their families, so I would like to describe one of my favorite interventions I used to do with groups.

Back when I worked in facilities, I developed a week-long exercise to help addicts learn about hope. On Monday, I would sit everyone down and explain that I had a task for them to complete. Each of them would receive one mustard seed. After handing out these incredibly small seeds, I gave them some instructions. First, they had to keep it with them at all times. Except for necessities like showering, it should always be on their person. In every group, I had them, and if I happened to see them in passing, I would make them check and see if they had it. If not, I would make them go find it if they had not lost it. Inevitably, people lost them. I remember one guy who lost his mustard seed five seconds after handing it to him. This was frustrating at the moment, but enlightening later on. If a mustard seed ever was lost, all they had to do was stop me and ask if they could have another. Without fail, the next group session that we had contained an argument about why I was making them keep this small seed around and how much of a pain it was to hold on to. I reiterated that losing the seed was not a problem. All they had to do was get help to find it or come to me for another. As the week went on, clients would begin to get creative, putting the seed in their nametags, small pockets, and even cigarette boxes with cellophane. Still, some would lose the mustard seed and learn that the rules were simple and all they needed to do was ask for help finding it or get a new one. Finally, Friday comes around. By this point, not only are my clients invested in this project, but other clients are wondering why their peers are doing such a stupid task.

Also, by Friday I would slyly look around the facility's grounds to make sure I didn't aid in an accidental planting of a mustard plant. It never happened, but there would be some interesting explanations to a supervisor that I would have to have come up with.

With everyone seated, I went around the room and allowed clients to guess the purpose of the exercise, as well as what they thought the mustard seed represented. Some thought it was an exercise in compliance and listening to authority. Still, others guessed that I was making them carry around their sobriety. Once I finally broke the news that their mustard seed represented hope for recovery, the questions began to flood, and lights began to turn on. One of the first questions I would get asked would be why I would give them something so small. They began to realize that this was all the hope they could fathom having. Apart from the shame motivator to force their hand, there was little room for much else. In their addiction and cycles of self-hatred, they had lost the ability to hope. Conversations then turned to where they ended up keeping the seeds. Many reported keeping them exactly where they would keep their drugs of choice. Little metaphorical explanation is needed here, I hope. Other clients would report needing to keep it always within their eyesight because they lose things so easily and forget where they left them. Again, no explanation is needed here. Among countless other analogies that were drawn, there is one that defines this whole exercise and can hopefully explain what is needed for addicts in early recovery.

Clients would then ask the million-dollar question: So why do you have a whole container of those seeds and we only get one?

Now, please hear me, this next part is not to fluff my sense of self or make it seem like I have some grand understanding about the meaning of life that they do not. Instead, it is to show a point that is applicable outside of the treatment setting.

To these clients, I state that I have a whole container of hope as I have spent years cultivating it. Over time, I have been able to see the blessings of recovery and the engagement that has come with relationships that fulfill and challenge me. In turn, this building of hope that I have becomes something I can share. When someone else needs hope, I have built and continue to build what is needed to stay healthy and progress in my own life. In metaphorical terms, I have become a hope broker. The hope for recovery that I give does not come from me. I have very little to give of myself. Instead, it is my job to help transition this process for others.

I remind clients again of what I said about the mustard seed and what they need to do if they lose it. All it takes is a sense of humility to ask for more, hoping that the hope that they receive blooms into something that can continually produce hope on its own. For now, I can give hope as needed, always attempting to be a light to point someone in a positive direction. However, they can only hold one mustard seed at the beginning of their journey, and they have to find a way to hold onto it for themselves, creating a way to hold onto hope for their journey forward.

PRINCIPLES OF VALUE

Another consistent concern that I see in practice is finding a sense of value. On the surface, this seems rather straightforward. People find value in relationships, beliefs, and ideas, right? Well, even for people without addiction, it is not that simple.

Let me paint a picture for you. We would all love to say that we value ourselves, or as the current cultural talking point is, we should love ourselves just the way we are. This sounds incredibly virtuous and positive on the surface. However, there are two main problems with this mantra. First, we as people tend to suck. Now, I know we have highlights of our lives and things that we do that we could point to, but if we were truly honest, in our times of distance and isolation from others, we often do and believe things against our advertised character. I truly believe that there has been a convincing veneer modern society has created that has been reinforced to attempt to assure us that we are beautiful just the way we are. For many, this has begun to set in so much that we begin to believe it ourselves. All the while, there is an undercurrent that keeps alive our secrets that we hide from everyone, even the ones we love. When someone shows that dark underbelly, we make judgments about that person, often asserting that it shows their true character. Still, we point these things out to push against our insecurities in the hope that this smokescreen will prevent others from seeing how bad we really are. As a result, we end up reinforcing unhealthy beliefs and behaviors to avoid criticism or conviction of our actions.

The other problem with this overt positivity and unyielding reinforcement is that I do not think we truly believe it. We may try to believe it about other people, but we have issues and insecurities and do not believe we are perfect the way we are. Much like the last problem, we lie to ourselves to convince ourselves and others that we are confident and successful. So, we end up sincerely deluding ourselves, becoming detached from our intimate understanding of our unique human condition. Then, we wonder why things are not working out or why we seem to be disconnected from our true feelings.

I hope by this point that you have gotten the message that addiction is not special. I have repeated it both literally and figuratively many times in this book. However, I will then apply this problem of value to addiction, and we can walk the addict's rationale alongside our own.

In response to this lack of a true value, which I call inherent value, addicts tend to harshly lean into a performative value. Let me define the two of these. Inherent value means that no matter the situation or behavior, a person has something worth engaging and fighting for. Just their mere existence is valuable. Performative value is the opposite. It focuses on doing what is necessary to obtain value, at the cost of never being able to rest on it. Performative value is both extremely engaging and corrosive. Like a treadmill, the addict feels the need to always prove themselves as worth something. This can be done through family relationships and expectations. A son can come to believe that his academic achievements are what makes him valuable to his parents, causing great anxiety. This child can truly come to believe that his parents will love him if he can get the right grades. Or a wife can find her value in her ability to connect to and be praised by her husband. Much like our previous chapter on codependency, someone may find it their goal to be supportive and loved. When they are not, they feel a loss of who they are and what they are worth.

For the addict, this performative value is taken a step further. One of the functions of addiction is to deal with what is overwhelming. In terms of value, this failure to obtain success in performative value leaves them hopeless. Instead of being able to get off this treadmill, they are chained to it and need to find a way to cope. For those that know about Greek mythology, there is a very helpful story we can use here. The god Sisyphus is most famous for the depiction of him pushing a rock up a hill. For poor Sisyphus, this is a punishment that was imposed upon him by Zeus. Due to his perceived transgressions, he was forced to push a boulder up a steep hill by the end of the day. If he were able to get it to the top, his punishment would be complete, but there was a catch. He was never able to reach the top and rest. Instead, he would get incredibly close and fail. The day would dawn again, and Sisyphus would have to go through the grueling process of seeing his shame in front of him, this boulder representing his failure to perform well enough to leave the cycle of shame he was in. Again he would push. This is another example of how to understand addiction, even if you have never experienced it yourself. The addict is cursed with the task of seeing their shame in front of them, a reminder of their failure. Still, their only ability to make things right is to push that boulder up the hill. This is what I call the Curse of Sisyphus in addiction.

Let us then consider what this may look like practically. Under the weight of all that someone has done wrong, they start to crumble emotionally. They become dejected and lost. Unfortunately, like what was discussed in an earlier chapter, addicts only have a few ways to deal with issues. For a lack of worth, that only option is to try to perform better. This is seen frequently when someone leaves treatment and immediately attempts to fix everything wrong with their lives and relationships, hoping to "perform" well enough to earn their life back. Others feel that all is hopeless and lost and can come into the world sober again with the constant strain of possibly never being enough. Amid active addiction, all of these things are present but are hidden. Behind all of the drugs, alcohol, and denial, is an overwhelming sense that they are not enough, they will never be enough, and their only option is to try anyway.

Amid active addiction, this performative value can come through a retort about how they do not feel loved or that they will never be good enough for someone. It can also be seen in the distancing from important loved ones or responsibilities. If you have to perform to get value, but you know that you will fail anyway, distance can create a cushion that dampens the effects of loss. Pushing away also leads to failure to perform, as an active addict will have moments of clarity and feel some of the weight of their failures and distance. The mother who is still using and is away from her children feels the Curse of Sisyphus when the drugs wear off, hoping that distance can ease the pain and disconnection can help prevent failure of the growth of their children since they are failures themselves. Maybe someone else has a better shot at filling a parental role as her cocaine use reminds them of her inevitable failure to provide what is needed.

For those who have not experienced addiction for themselves, this can also be a familiar feeling. Have you ever become so emotionally invested in your work that any criticism or possible sense of failure brings up more emotion that should be relevant? Do you feel that you have to be a good enough spouse, parent, or friend to receive affection and connection from others? For those more spiritual, is there a constant drive to be good enough to a higher power or calling, that if you are good enough, you will be accepted and cared for? We often are not able to easily recognize these things as our sense of control gives us a purpose. If you are a good enough employee, they cannot fire you. If you are a good enough spouse, they will not leave you or cheat. If you are a good enough follower of a particular faith, it does not matter what they think, you are in control of what happens. Vulnerability and inherent value are not needed.

If you have missed it this far, I will say this again. Addicts are not special. You feel much of the same things they do. They simply feel these fears and pains to a more severe degree than you may. Performative value will rot away at our sense of self. To some degree, we all feel the Curse of Sisyphus. We all fight for some vain grasp at controlling a world that is unable to be predicted or considered completely safe. This is a part of our human condition, something we must learn to overcome.

The opposite of this performance that dictates what we are worth is inherent value. Be aware, the belief that every person contains a value in their existence is something that may be more controversial than you may initially realize. Much of this belief has become tribalistic. You see, our group is beautiful and amazing just the way they are, but that group over there has something screwy in their head and should just leave. In general speech, many find themselves giving lip service to the idea that everyone has a place in this world and should be treated with respect. That is unless some person or group of people has become so detached that they are no longer human, but a statistic. They are just a group of people not worth considering. Following an inherent sense of value to its logical end, everyone has to have a value worth seeing. The felon, the terrorist, the bigot, the odd, the outcast, the hateful, the sick, and the addict all have to have some spark inside of them worth latching onto. Granted this may be a radical idea but working with addiction and severe shame is rather radical. Many times in my office, men and women have found their faces in their hands, weeping over their stolen identity and innocence or even how they have become so tainted by their trespasses that they do not deserve love or a kind word. If you hope to truly reach out to all addicts, you must come to believe that everyone has a sense of value, something worth fighting for.

What is counter to addiction is not trying hard enough to push the boulder to the top of the hill, but the acceptance that with some tether to the outside world, love and value are given inherently. Now, you may recoil at the idea that the active addict needs to find a sense of value. They seem entitled to everyone's time and money. Do they not think so highly of themselves that they should take themselves down a peg? It may seem that way on the surface, but it is not true. They feel the need to suck the life and value out of those around them as they feel so devoid of meaningful substance, it is all they can think of doing. From a sense of inherent value comes an inevitable result, the desire to be different. Many correlate an inherent value to a secure identity. If an addict were to think they have worth, their lives would not be chained to the pursuit of finding worth in their performance, and life begins to have meaning. He really could be an amazing father, supporting his children in their turmoil. On a solid foundation, a home can be built. It can even be worth developing and struggling through.

There are many places to find this inherent value. Some find it in faith and others find it in family or relationships. Still, others will find it in solid truths of the world or the past. The potential of the future can even provide some comfort. As this is not a book of spiritual implication, I will leave that up to the reader to decide what that means to them. Whatever this sense of meaning is that is significant enough for the addict to latch onto, it must be something that is either concretely or mostly immovable. If someone is connected to a higher power that is always with them and always cares for them, that can work. If another uses the office of a parent, spouse, or loving friend as a way to connect to inherent value, that can also be useful. I would recommend multiple tethers. The more points of foundation that we have, the more stable we feel in our sense of self. Tragedy may strike the wife and cause a possible relapse if her only tether was being a spouse. With only one tether that can be broken, there is not much option.

For each individual, these tethers of inherent value should give one overall message. Just as you exist, you have value. This does not mean you are absolved of any wrongdoing or that you are unable to be criticized. Inherent value also does not negate the need to make drastic changes and admit that there is much to adapt to. Instead, inherent value should bring comfort and conviction. Yes, this sense of value should keep someone stable, but it should also push them to live differently from their addiction. It can both encourage recovery and be a result of recovery. As a mother, you have a great need to connect and love your children. You will always be their mother and have some influence in their lives. That does not give you the right to abuse that relationship, even though it is irreparably broken at the moment. Instead, inherent value should boost you to become something that you are proud of, something that gives you life and fills those around you as well.

Finding Deeper Issues

Without fail, there is something that has always come true for clients that stick through the process of therapy. Addiction is never the core issue. It is the result of years of issues and unresolved hurts coming to a boiling point. I am not going to delve into the specifics of theoretical insight here, but I will say that within the walls of my office, everyone's addiction makes sense. There is a true, legitimate reason that someone does something so ridiculous as to risk everything that they love for some fleeting feeling of euphoria.

Be careful reading further. Even as I am writing this, I can feel my own emotions creeping into my throat. Maybe it's the heartfelt music I am listening to while writing or even the result of sitting in my chair to type this book out. To be completely honest, what I will speak about next is something that I treat with great reverence. What can be perceived as hallowed ground for many is the true nature of their soul, the details of how their pain has come to pass. I do not assert that I am some sage or hold great power to peer into the souls of others. Much of the work that I do is sitting at the moment and helping clients feel and understand their own experiences. Still, what I thought would be some great moment of elation and excitement in discovering the function of addiction in an individual, ends up not feeling that way at all. More of this will be discussed later.

Here I will tell you the story of someone we will call Rebecca. Know that what you will read cannot hope to encompass the complexity of her person. Please do not assume that treatment and healing are as simple as connecting past events. Into the more common forms of addiction, which tend to be sporadic but debilitating, she found herself unable to control her drinking and cocaine use. These concerns continued to creep up, and the use increased. Many would find this to be something they could endure, but Rebecca needed a change. So, she reached out, and we started meeting. She was always incredibly polite and curious about how everything fits together for her.

After introductions and understanding her history, we started to notice some trends. At first, there were these unrelated patterns that seemed more interesting than meaningfully connected. There was a time of sexual exploration and swinging through boyfriends, only to get hurt time and time again. There was also this continued desire to be chosen. This was seen through her family life, as well as the way that she maintained relationships. Rebecca also sought comfort in her family and wanted to make sure that her family name was upheld. At the time of our initial sessions, she was with a man who honestly treated her terribly. I cannot come out and say that someone's significant other is toxic at the beginning of the therapeutic relationship. Without trust and hope for change, most people will just stop seeking help. So, sometimes as a therapist, I have to bide my time and allow clients to discover things on their own.

We also found patterns in her drinking. When she would be out with friends, it would increase, but not go overboard. However, when Mr. Perfect was there, all bets were off. Drinking beer was like breathing air, except she was hyperventilating. With this increase in alcohol usually came cocaine. This became a great cause of concern for her and me as well. Over time and considerable effort on her part in therapy, Rebecca was able to understand what she was feeling and thinking minutes, hours, and even days before an episode of drinking or cocaine use. She could even detail every interaction before and after and was able to see herself in the midst of it. Rebecca made progress, but there was still something left over.

After realizing that her enabler was not helpful and did not desire to change, she finally broke things off. That should have fixed it, right? It did not. To be fair, her life and emotions did significantly improve. He was finally gone, and she could be single and happy until he came to mind, and she was lonely. He also visited her once, even after breaking up. Like a gust of icy wind, she tumbled back into drinking spells and cocaine use. Rebecca could see who triggered her drinking, every emotion leading up to it, and even how she was vulnerable to her past experience and the week prior. Then, once her brain had finally caught up to her heart and she was out in the open, something amazing happened.

During one session, Rebecca told me that there was more I needed to know. She had been assaulted when she was a teenager, by someone close to her that could even still speak to her. Through a nearly blank stare, she recounted the details of the assault. Rebecca was even able to rationalize why she never said anything.

At that moment, she looked at me and wondered why it seemed as if she was a lost girl and unable to feel the pain that was locked away. From there, her story and her treatment-resistant addiction made sense.

Please know that I am about to tell someone's sacred story. Details were changed and information was shuffled, but at the heart, this is someone's beginning stages of addiction. From this pain came ways she tried to cope. Rebecca went on to try to understand her trauma by controlling relationships through sexual encounters. What she called sexual preference ended up being a way for her to make sense of and take back what she had lost, her childhood innocence. Over time, these attempts failed, and she continued to try to be chosen by men, to be special enough to be protected and cared for. Coupled with this lack of vulnerability in sexual relationships, Rebecca also found herself needing a reminder that she was worthy of who she was with. When these relationships ultimately failed, Rebecca sank further into her pain. You see, after trying to control trauma for a long time, the desire to be whole again does not go away, but the confidence in asserting your needs does. With this pain still needing an outlet and age eroding her confidence, she found herself a tall, dark, and handsome man. The boyfriend she recently broke up with during our sessions was much different than she expected. He was detached and assumed his sexual desires trumped any need for connection or intimacy.

Unfortunately for Rebecca, her trauma followed her from her childhood. The pain and unresolved sadness carried decades, hoping to find a place to be healed. Instead, she ended up dating a man that resembled the genesis of her struggles in life, a cold and selfish man who took something from her. This is where her addiction took over. Mostly subconscious, but able to be verified in sessions later, Rebecca realized something. Her addiction came from the unresolved pain that festered deep within her. After all those years, she was unable to make things right and had to live with the only type of man she felt worthy of. Despair that would have drowned anyone started to take Rebecca, and drinking made these feelings seem less consuming.

This was a pivotal moment for Rebecca. She was finally able to piece together why she had seen her increase in drinking and how it came about. It was never about the boyfriend himself, but what he represented, what she relived every time she was with him. Many addicts dream of this insight. Others would want to know why they do what they do as well. To the reader, this may have seemed like a wonderful occasion. We know what caused it! We can work on that! Healing is just around the corner!

I will tell you that from my experience, excitement is never the case. Coming face-to-face with the genesis of your addiction is never something clients are excited to see. Many would even assume that even a smile would come about. Instead, the walk into the pain that paved years of travel is a rather somber occasion. For Rebecca, underneath the layers of trauma, life experience, personal choices, and unfortunate circumstances was a sad little girl that wondered why something terrible happened to her. Her life and story were not a puzzle to be solved. I often feel a tinge of excitement, and then sorrow washes me over as clients see what lies underneath all their questions, what lies in the silence. Little is known of someone's soul from answering a therapist's questions. Not much can be expected in an interview. Instead, when distraction is put away, trauma is understood, and humanity is experienced, the silence shows us what we are. Beyond the chaos of drinking, cocaine use, unhealthy boyfriends, and constant interruptions, Rebecca could see herself.

I hope this for you, as well. Whether you are the addict yourself, the loved one, or someone who is just seeking to find themselves, I wish that you could find a place where you can truly see yourself and see your pain. I would love for everyone to be able to face their demons and be able to find healing. Sadly, I am not sure how many do. Trips like these are arduous, and few dare to begin them. You must be able to see things through and find the sup-

port you need to not only recognize your struggles but have the
strength to work on them and find a new self.

Getting Help

At this point, many are looking for practical advice, a way to find
the next steps in their recovery or the support of others who desperately need it. While I usually do not give direct advice, I will
make an allowance here to hopefully guide you on your way.
Know that what I will give you is somewhat general and should
not be taken as absolute advice but can hopefully provide the direction needed to understand what to do next.

For medical concerns, there are both short and long-term factors to consider. First, there may be immediate medical needs affecting daily health, but also risk factors related to the type of substance used. If an addict is using any kind of street drug, there is
no guarantee that what they believe they are taking is really what
they think it is. What is assumed to be cocaine could easily contain
traces of drywall dust or even fentanyl. With all substances, illic-
it or legal, there will be a withdrawal period when drug or alcohol
use stops. If you are planning an intervention, know that this will
be something to be mindful of and plan for. For some substances,
there can be either severe or deadly consequences for an abrupt
stoppage of use. Speak to a medical professional that can advise
on the next steps.

Shortly after use, addicts can have a wide range of symptoms to
deal with from restlessness, anxiety, and body pain. These should
also be considered as their brain knows that more of their drug
of choice will soothe their pain. In the long term, medical consequences can range anywhere from organ failure to heart attack,
and even permanent brain damage. There will likely be some effects that linger. Other medical needs could relate to how the brain
processes hormones related to stress management and happiness.
While no one should consider medication a cure-all, addicts need
a fighting chance to make a choice. Medicine should provide clarity and opportunity, not detachment.

For the addict and their loved ones, therapy is a must. Everyone in this system has been traumatized by addiction. Each person may process it in their own way, but no one gets out of this clean. If possible, have joined therapy sessions with multiple members of a supportive family or friends to teach trust and communication, and relearn how to interact. If children are involved, they will likely need significant support in therapy since they learned about the world from their parents and will need guidance in a new way of living. It may be beneficial for some families to have sessions with multiple generations to give insight into what they would like to see and how much they care for one another. If the addict is married or has a long-term committed partner, couples therapy should be encouraged to help break the bonds of addiction and create a new understanding. Some may see this as an opportunity to heal everyone, while others may see this as a good time to move on. Either way, healthy lives are the goal.

Many addicts and their families find support in the community and spiritual groups. While it is not necessary to be connected to a religious institution, resources and support groups tend to have some tether to a church or faith community. If this is your direction or something you are considering, I would urge you to not just fill a seat. I have not heard of anyone who has gained a new purpose in life by being somewhat present. There are two points I hope you consider. The first is that people, in a detached sense, are terrible. Religious organizations house people who suck. People will be hypocrites and hateful everywhere. Find a small community wherever you go and take the message and beliefs over what your neighbor has to say in gossip about the couple next door. The other point is that simple involvement is not enough. Many of those in recovery spoke to me about how their experience in groups was awful because no one spoke to them or tried to see how their day was. Inevitably, they never asked anyone else as well. If you want to see if any of that stuff is true, do not just haphazardly involve yourself; integrate and see what happens.

My final piece of direction is that growth looks much more like an ascending mountain range than a curve. Trending upwards is certainly the goal and a deep dive to previous depths is not ideal. Instead understand that there will be wins and losses, at times having only hope to hold on to. What you have taken away from this book is not concrete but a guide. Those with decades of recovery may disagree with my points, and that is okay. There is no one way to get sober and healthy. Instead of just taking my word for it, speak to people around you who have seen and been successful in recovery. Hope for the future, and fight for one another. In the end, your health and sobriety need to matter, or you may lose your life along the way. You may need to find where you left it.

CONCLUSION

WE FINALLY COME to the end. To finish this book, I will give a small word to those who may be reading this. I pray these small letters give you some comfort in whatever you decide is your path forward. You hold something precious but weighty here. I call this feeling the Burden of Knowing. There is no returning to ignorance or blissful misunderstanding. You cannot go back, no matter how much you may try. I would also like to thank you for taking the time to hear my thoughts. I am writing this with no expectation that anyone will read it. At a minimum, it is a way to organize my thoughts and give clients a way to remain grounded in their journey. If this has been helpful to you, please share this book and your personal story with them so that they may find a way to hope for their future.

TO THE SPOUSE OR PARTNER

The ever-enduring partner, you may have the most difficult role of anyone related to an addict. There have been years of concern which led to sleepless nights and running on fumes. You have made excuses and covered for them many times, hoping it will be the last. It would be all too easy to just walk away, but you can't. Something keeps you connected. Maybe it is the hope that they are in there somewhere, or maybe it is the need to keep life as stable as possible for yourself and the kids.

To you, I wish for your emotional and physical health, not that it has to be apart from your spouse. The best chance they have at recovery is you becoming healthy yourself and holding healthy boundaries. Out of love, desperation, or the last shred of energy you have left, be whole. Find love in things you have lost. Go to people who love you and miss the spark that you lost so long ago. If the addict in your life is willing to see hope and embrace change, you can decide whether to do the same. Addiction itself is abandonment and a way to force a partner's hand. I hope that you find a way to decide the next steps for yourself and your children.

To the Child

If you can only take one thing from this book, please know this. There is nothing you can do to change them. Your parent may find hope and support from you and may even use a relationship with you as motivation. Unfortunately, this will never be enough. No matter what you do either physically or relationally, you cannot make them well again. This is not your burden to bear, and you hold no blame.

To you, I wish that you could let go of trying to control enough or be enough to make either one of your parents okay. Their relationship rests on their shoulders, not yours. There may never come a day when sobriety arrives. I pray it does. If it does not, release yourself from the weight of trying to make things okay. Break the cycle of addiction and unhealthy relationships for yourself and your own family. You need healing as well. Children are often the overlooked part of the effects of addiction. Even as adults, there can be gaping relational wounds that need love and support. You have the permission to feel everything granted to you and do whatever is needed to keep this sickness from continuing. Honor them by being well yourself.

To the Parent

Your child has slowly withered away. Much of what made them your baby has disappeared, overtaken by drugs or alcohol until only the influence of a chemical remains. After fighting for many years, you may have found yourself full of guilt and shame about how you must have messed them up in your parenting or some-how caused this catastrophe. You have undoubtedly heard every-one's opinion and worked every possible outcome of this already.

To you, I wish peace in your next steps. Whatever comes about next will take so much time to see progress. You may be the only hope that your child has for recovery. Most will give up on them, and the only ones left are there to enable their addiction. I also hope you find others like you, those that also want to see their chil-dren well. However, one of the most difficult decisions may be in front of you. If you have come to a point where the only option is to let them go, do so with caution and conviction. You will always love them and as much as they argue otherwise, they know that too. Your child has grown up and will have to make some gut-wrench-ing decisions. Let them be the adult they need to be.

To the Loved One

You are in a difficult spot. There is a chance that you could be one of the only people who care enough to stick around. You could also be one of the last enablers in their life. Friends are often dis-connected from family conversations and only get the part of the story that benefits the addict. Remember who you are to them. You are a friend or family member who wants to see them well. En-courage connection and growth where possible in their family as well.

To you, I hope you find solidarity in your own life. Addiction takes from everyone around it. Through manipulation and shame, it drains life and will out of everyone connected. Your own life and well-being have likely suffered. Your relationships may have felt the effects of this unhealthy person. You can provide a role model of healthy living and boundaries by keeping them accountable. They may look to you when others push them away. Let them know you love them, and keep yourself well.

To the Addict

From the length or intensity of this book, you may have come to believe that I am hyper-critical of addicts. It may have been from the way I spoke about boundaries or how abrupt I am about what is needed from people to push towards lives worth living. If I can be honest one more time, hear me. This book is for you. Yes, it is much about how family members and loved ones can make sense of things. As much as addicts have yelled and berated me for what I have asked of them, what their family members needed, or what research is showing us about addiction, these words are out of love.

To you, I pray for exhaustion and surrender. Admit that your life and sanity are falling apart, and stop fighting. Quit pushing against vulnerability and honesty with those that care about you. None of this will be easy or pleasant, but you do not know how much time you have left. There is no guarantee that you will live long enough to finish reading this page. End this constant battle against yourself that only fuels your inner shame. Give way to those that can help and listen. Take time to sit in silence and see what is there. Have enough hope to fill a mustard seed, and sit in silence often. Your life will probably never go back to the way that it was, and many years of struggle lie ahead of you. Your journey will be grueling, and you will want to relapse many times. Do it anyway. It is worth it. It was for me, and I hope it will be for you too.

DR. TRAVIS THOMPSON, LMFT holds a PhD and is a Licensed Marriage and Family Therapist, host of the Bold Lines podcast from Murfreesboro, TN. Just south of Nashville, Travis has seen many different ways that addiction has brought to his community. His clinical and academic work focuses on how addiction impacts systems of people, from couples, to families, to communities. Travis combines compassion and honesty to provide those he works with the opportunity to find healing and growth.

For more information, contact:
TRAVISTHOMPSONMEDIA@HOTMAIL.COM

INDEX

A

ANXIETY, ANXIOUS 11, 23, 28, 36, 56, 59, 71, 72, 97, 98, 120, 126, 138, 139, 145, 149, 158, 163, 164, 175, 182, 193

ATTACHMENT, ATTACHMENTS 23, 25, 27, 28, 29, 30, 31, 32, 61, 161

B

BELIEFS, BELIEF, BELIEVE 11, 23, 28, 36, 56, 59, 71, 72, 97, 98, 120, 126, 138, 139, 145, 149, 158, 163, 164, 175, 182, 193

BRAIN 12, 13, 14, 15, 16, 17, 18, 19, 20, 21, 22, 24, 28, 37, 39, 57, 58, 62, 189, 192

C

CHILDREN, CHILD ix, 3, 14, 23, 24, 25, 26, 27, 28, 32, 39, 45, 47, 48, 69, 87, 90, 95, 96, 97, 98, 99, 100, 101, 102, 103, 104, 105, 106, 108, 109, 110, 111, 112, 113, 115, 120, 121, 122, 123, 124, 125, 126, 129, 131, 132, 133, 141, 145, 149, 157, 167, 185, 186, 187, 193, 196, 197

CONSEQUENCES 2, 3, 6, 12, 17, 19, 45, 49, 53, 56, 62, 67, 76, 83, 84, 91, 96, 97, 104, 105, 127, 143, 144, 165, 171, 173, 192

COPE, COPING 10, 28, 37, 39, 40, 67, 69, 108, 109, 113, 120, 121, 156, 168, 173, 183, 190

D

DEPRESSION 8, 9, 11, 36, 40, 41, 42, 52, 55, 57, 79

F

FAITH 4, 5, 144, 179, 185, 186, 193

G

GOD 149, 172, 183

GROWTH xi, 17, 49, 50, 55, 72, 97, 102, 130, 148, 154, 155, 185, 193, 197, 199

H

HOPE ix, x, xi, xii, 1, 5, 13, 29, 32, 33, 35, 36, 42, 47, 48, 52, 53, 60, 71, 72, 74, 79, 85, 89, 93, 107, 108, 112, 115, 116, 117, 120, 121, 126, 128, 132, 137, 138, 144, 149, 150, 151, 152, 153, 156, 158, 159, 163, 165, 166, 167, 170, 172, 174, 175, 179, 180, 181, 182, 183, 186, 188, 189, 191, 193, 194, 195, 196, 197, 198

L

LOVE vii, ix, 17, 20, 41, 48, 49, 55, 74, 75, 93, 106, 109, 110, 134, 162, 170, 172, 173, 182, 183, 186, 187, 188, 191, 196, 197, 198

M

MARRIAGE 11, 53, 100, 125, 132, 134, 140, 141, 145
MOOD 8, 37, 42, 43

P

PARENTS, PARENT ix, 15, 22, 26, 47, 52, 69, 95, 96, 97, 98, 99, 100, 101, 102, 103, 104, 105, 107, 108, 109, 112, 113, 115, 120, 121, 122, 123, 124, 125, 129, 130, 131, 167, 183, 193, 196
POWER xi, 4, 54, 88, 91, 95, 124, 185, 187, 188
PROGRAM 2, 3, 4, 12, 90, 132
PSYCHOLOGICAL x, xi, 9, 10, 16, 23, 31, 36, 65, 161

R

RECOVERY ix, 114, 139, 163, 170, 173
RESEARCH xi, xii, 2, 4, 5, 6, 9, 11, 12, 13, 23, 25, 43, 68, 82, 84, 96, 97, 111, 129, 156, 198
RESPONSIBLE, RESPONSIBILITY 16, 53, 54, 89, 95, 113, 115, 140

S

SEPARATION 26, 27, 30, 31
SUBSTANCE 5, 6, 7, 19, 31, 35, 36, 37, 38, 39, 40, 41, 42, 43, 52, 53, 55, 57, 58, 59, 60, 62, 63, 66, 67, 68, 69, 72, 77, 79, 112, 113, 128, 134, 161, 192
SYMPTOM, SYMPTOMS 5, 6, 7, 19, 31, 35, 36, 37, 38, 39, 40, 41, 42, 43, 52, 53, 55, 57, 58, 59, 60, 62, 63, 66, 67, 68, 69, 72, 77, 79, 112, 113, 128, 134, 161, 192

T

THERAPY v, i, ii, 72, 89, 94, 151, 175

TRAUMA 10, 16, 29, 55, 56, 57, 60, 65-80, 102, 108, 114, 126, 129, 155, 157, 160, 164, 165, 170, 190, 191

V

VALUE 2, 29, 41, 45, 115, 145, 182, 183, 184, 185, 186, 187

W

WORRY x, 102

www.ingramcontent.com/pod-product-compliance
Lightning Source LLC
Chambersburg PA
CBHW011537260326
41914CB00036B/1973/J